Building faith in
the Christadelphian
community.

TIDINGS

Volume 85, Number 9 / October, 2022

SPECIAL ISSUE

ECCLESIAL DIFFERENCES IN THE ONE BODY

By Dave Jennings

The Tidings Publishing Committee would like to draw our reader's attention to this month's editorial, which focuses on Biblical principles to consider in dealing with issues where there is a diversity of opinion not addressed expressly in our Statement of Faith.

IT must have been painful for Jewish believers to contemplate the differences introduced by new Gentile converts in emerging ecclesias. Was it possible that salvation did not require all of the essential rituals and traditions they believed were associated with a holy life? Generations of faithful Jews had defined holiness by these commandments. The observant Jew, now a believer in Jesus Christ, still saw these practices as Divine decrees as well as differentiation of Abraham's seed. The practice of the Law of Moses was integral to Jewish culture. It was how commerce was governed and justice administered. The Law united God's people, even when they were under captivity by a foreign nation.

However, new Gentile converts required a rethinking of the Law. Many eyewitnesses of Gentile converts were blessed with Spirit gifts. They were authentic believers, yet they were not observing the Law. Was this an error that "stronger" believers must correct? Should Gentile converts be taught to keep the Law? How about circumcision and the observance of the Sabbath? What about dietary practices? Did God expect all Gentile believers to become practicing Jews?

I wonder if we can try to place ourselves in these difficult discussions long ago. Some would argue that the practices of the Law were timeless. God commanded His people to keep these observances as a "statute forever." Didn't Moses teach that these Laws were requirements of His people? How was it that Gentiles could be saved and not embrace these practices?

Practice and Principle

Looking back 2,000 years, we can see that the overwhelming message of gospel growth was unity in diversity. There would be vast differences in practice from one ecclesia to another. There was no conformity to a single way of worship. If one attended a meeting in Jerusalem, it included deeply observant Jews, who believed fully in Jesus but kept the Law. Even the Apostle Paul, while spending most of his time outside Judea, made provisions for observing the feasts of the Law. A meeting of brothers and sisters in Antioch, Corinth, Galatia, or Cilicia would have looked far different than those in Jerusalem. How would these vastly dissimilar practices enable the growth and development of one body of Christ across the Roman world?

We might assume that if one agrees to the same Scriptural principles as us, they will follow uniformity in practice. But this has rarely been true in the body of Christ. We see multiple examples where agreement on principle existed, but there was a variation in practice to accommodate local needs. For example, Gentile and Jewish believers agreed an idol was nothing but wood or stone. In cities like Corinth, some members would have a deep aversion to anything tainted with the idol worship they had once practiced. Therefore, some chose to refrain from eating food offered to an idol. However, others did eat, recognizing there was nothing wrong with consuming the food. The real issue wasn't the practice but the principle. It wasn't right or wrong to eat food offered to an idol, but the principle was about the impact eating the meat would have on the brother or sister whose conscience was wounded. Principle always trumps practice. Get the principle right, and it will govern practice.

Ecclesias today have learned to agree on principles but also accept that there are some areas where we can follow very different practices. The issue of marriage and divorce is one such area. I don't believe there is any ecclesia that would not accept the principle that marriage is intended for life, and the LORD hates divorce. Yet, there is no uniformity among ecclesias on handling matters of divorce. One may disagree with the practice of another ecclesia, but in the end, it is a choice made in love when we remain committed to being united as a body of Christ. It is possible to agree on the principle while accepting that not all brethren see appropriate practice the same way as I do?

The Jerusalem Conference Solution

All one has to do is examine the famous Jerusalem Conference of Acts 15 to see the spectrum of opinions in the body of Christ. There were men of Judaea who argued one *"cannot be saved"* unless they are circumcised. (v. 1). Pharisee believers also argued this issue was about much more than circumcision; it required all believers everywhere to keep all of the Law. Some wanted a directive sent to all ecclesias, stating it was *"needful to circumcise them and to command them to keep the law of Moses."* (v. 5). Peter, who received the thrice-repeated vision of unclean animals on a sheet in Joppa, had previously been rebuked by Paul in Antioch (Gal 2:11-17) for withdrawing himself from the Gentiles in fear of the party of the circumcision. Paul and Barnabas delivered a stirring account of the miracles and wonders God had wrought among the Gentiles by them. What a fascinating array of deeply held experiences and views!

Today, we may see the appropriate answer to this debate. But of course, we have the benefit of the direction of the Spirit through James (Acts 15:13-21) and two millennia of experience. In reality, the Jerusalem Conference may have been the most crucial example of brethren respectfully and lovingly working through conflict in New Testament times.

Bro. Alfred D. Norris (1914-2003) of England once pointed out that the principle of the Jerusalem Conference was that Gentile believers didn't need to become Jews, but they did need to stop pagan practices. Practicing diversity was accepted as long as it was consistent with the principles taught by our Lord. With the Jerusalem Conference, we see an example of how unity was appealed

for and not demanded. Permitting ecclesias to make their own decisions locally accomplished this goal. Despite having the greatest Christian thinkers at the Conference and having the benefit of Spirit gifts, the communication to the ecclesias was not a mandate. Rather, the phrasing was: *"it seemed good unto us,"* and *"for it seemed good to the Holy Ghost, and to us."* (Acts 15:25, 28). It was a recommendation, though doubtless a compelling one. As the letter traveled around to ecclesias in Antioch, Syria, and Cilicia, the brethren would have been most pleased to receive it, as it detangled a significant and divisive issue they had been facing. This solution may have been more difficult for the ecclesias that subscribed to the doctrine of circumcision. Some may have followed the practice suggested in the letter; others we know did not. But there was no edict, no assumption that a centralized body would "command" a given practice. Even with such a significant difference, the only mandate was that the community be united.

Of course, some (mainly in Judea) never accepted the Conference's recommendation. Sadly, some of them traveled throughout the Roman world in an attempt to drive compliance with their point of view. This effort created immense disturbances in ecclesias, and undoubtedly, some individuals were lost because of the upset. The Apostle Paul and his co-workers had labored diligently to teach the critical principles of the Truth, only to have influential brethren from Judaea assert their faith was not built on knowledge. This became a ruthless campaign to make the gospel and its practice the same for all believers everywhere. The work of the Spirit prevailed by demonstrating that brethren should learn to live with difference in practice. Alignment of thinking about the gospel was essential. But variation in how to practice the gospel was permitted, as long as was consistent with Scriptural principles.

Today, some may feel our fellowship cannot have ambiguity in practice. Those who embrace this view think all ecclesias should operate with uniformity of practice, at least on the most important issues. This view is held not solely because of personal preference but from a genuine belief that salvation could be at risk. However, what united the ecclesias was the principle involved in the consideration. What had Christ taught? How was this principle intended to govern the behavior of believers? In some cases, the principle allowed for differences in practice. Throughout the first century, ecclesias were distinguished by differences, yet fellowship survived, even thrived, despite having significant variations in practice.

Damnable Heresies vs. Wholesome Doctrine

Later, *"damnable heresies"* would arise (2 Pet 2:1), but these were not due to differences in practice between the ecclesias. The primary threat came from corrupting philosophies of the world and erroneous heresies from within (Judaizers), which had wormed their way into the community. Some taught that Jesus was someone other than who he really was. The Gnostics believed in *"docetism,"* that is, they claimed he hadn't come in the flesh; John labels this as *"the spirit of antichrist."* (1 John 4:3). In those cases, they were to admonish the individuals teaching these errors. If the erring teachers didn't cease their promulgation of that teaching, they were to remove them as teachers and, in some cases, withdraw from them. But even then, the conflict between brethren was to be handled in love. In the Apocalypse, the Lord assessed Ephesus as having neglected their first love when fighting against such errors. (Rev 2:2-5).

The focus of the apostles and first century elders was to teach the wholesome gospel, correct doctrinal errors, and invite the community to identify Scriptural principles for their practices. In Corinth, the Breaking of Bread had devolved into an extremely non-spiritual practice for some. Paul educated them about the principle of what the Breaking of Bread was about and helped them see the folly of their existing customs. Paul also corrected the Corinthians about their practice of not addressing and resolving unrepented sin. He admonished them for failing to confront the sin of the brother who had his father's wife. But, instead of just demanding adherence, he reminded them of the threat of gangrene to the membership and how they were to behave to recover this man. Once there was alignment between teaching and principles, ecclesias were to ensure similar alignment for practice. It was their duty in Corinth, not to be assumed by other ecclesias.

> In Corinth, the Breaking of Bread had devolved into an extremely non-spiritual practice for some.

God's Grace is Sufficient

We know the failure of some to adopt the tenets of the Jerusalem Conference letter resulted in significant stress to ecclesias, certainly up to AD 70. As we sit here today, we would have strongly advised the party of the circumcision to accept the advice of the Counsel and implement its recommendations. But this was not the way of the Spirit. The way of the Spirit was for brethren with strongly different opinions to find a common way to work together for the gospel's sake. Some have suggested that Paul's *"thorn in the flesh"* (2 Cor 12:7-8), from which he prayed for relief, was about these same Jews pushing for complete compliance of all believers to keep the Law. We can imagine how this must have desperately confused novice believers and brought much pain to Paul and his co-workers. However, the message to Paul was, despite praying three times for relief, *"My grace is sufficient for thee."* (2 Cor12:9).

Paul was learning to acknowledge that God was in complete control. He would provide Paul and the ecclesias with what was needed to make it through the challenges to their faith. That's a helpful way to look at the differences between brethren.

This thought is a timeless principle for all believers. Rather than calcifying positions and polarizing a community, the message to Paul was to trust in the Lord. It is he who walks *"in the midst of the seven golden candlesticks."* (Rev 2:1). The introductory chapters to the Apocalypse demonstrate to us that our Lord is not only fully aware of what is happening in our ecclesias, but he has an accurate assessment of what needs to be done. It is always best to recognize that whatever challenges we face, his *"grace is sufficient."*

Cookie Cutter Solutions?

What would have happened if this difference of opinion between the circumcision party and the brethren assembled in Acts 15 had become siloed and uncooperative? Undoubtedly, it would not have been in the best interest of the spread of the true gospel. It's interesting to note that when Paul writes from Rome to Colossi, he mentions, *"Jesus, which is called Justus. These are the only men of the circumcision among my fellow workers for the kingdom of God, and they have been a comfort to me."* (Col 4:11 ESV). While the party of the circumcision had caused the Apostle great difficulties, he found a way to work productively with these brethren, who held very different views. It teaches us men of opposing views can find a common bond in the work of the Truth. This must be our goal.

As we consider fellowship today, we can learn much from our first century brethren. Throughout history, the body of Christ generally has never had a "cookie-cutter" approach to practice. It certainly is not today. When we look across our community, we see a wide variation of practices; some we may agree with, and others we may not. The essential requirement is that we have alignment on the *"doctrine of Christ."* (Heb 6:1). We embrace the principles of Christ, and we must allow for some variation of practice. While we can't permit the teachings of Scripture to be compromised, the unity in diversity principle between believers is equally essential today.

We are seeing our Lord moving to make rapid changes in our community. In the past twenty-five years, there has been unprecedented growth in many countries, and we are much richer spiritually for this outcome. We've realized the ability to preach the Word through the Internet, which has opened a window of opportunity to send our message to people and places we had never dreamed of. Surely, this is the Lord's work to help us remain strong as we face the challenges of the Last Days. May it be that we walk in unity together, seeking common ground on the teachings and principles of Christ, while we embrace our diversity as brothers and sisters.

Dave Jennings

YOUNG, SINGLE,
AND CHRISTADELPHIAN

By Kate Russell

IN the last year, the number of times my singleness has been commented on has grown significantly. In many respects, this is natural. I'm young, just 22, involved in my ecclesia, and many of my friends have recently gotten married. At this point, however, these comments have long ceased to feel like loving curiosity. At any age, they would be hurtful.

Here are a few examples of the remarks I'm referring to. I have been asked by peers and people outside my age group (sometimes by people I barely know) why I am still single. I've been encouraged to pursue relationships with some already in relationships. I've been pressured to join *Tinder*. I've been told to lower my expectations and standards, or I'll be single for the rest of my life. I've been told I would be a great couple with "so-and-so," only to find out the only reasons we would make great life partners are "because you're both single" or "you're both Christadelphians."

I've tried to understand the motives behind these comments. After all, I know the people saying these things care about me and these comments come from a place of love and a desire for me to be happy. With that mindset, I would like to provide, with an equal expression of love, an additional perspective on how to view singleness.

Happiness Is...

To say that my brothers and sisters make these remarks from a desire for me to be happy implies a heavy, hurtful message. It assumes that as a young, single sister, I am **not** happy and cannot be so until I'm no longer single. I highly doubt this is a conscious message, and I don't think this meaning would even occur to the person stating it. However, it appears that the vast majority of comments about my singleness come from people who are not single. Based on this, I often think that people in relationships tend to view people like me with pity. (I've been guilty of this myself.) Because I am single, I must be miserable.

But here's the thing; I'm not! I'm so far from being unhappy that being viewed as such takes me aback. I have so many loved ones, including family, friends, and brothers and sisters. I don't lack love in any respect. I've got a job I love, hobbies that bring me joy, and most importantly, a life dedicated to serving a God who loves me regardless of my relationship status.

Perhaps, as a community, we should re-evaluate how we view the single members of our body. Maybe when we read Paul's words on the subject in 1 Corinthians 7, we are too dismissive. Paul writes, *"But I say to the unmarried and to the widows: It is good for them if they remain even as I am."* (1 Cor 7:8 NKJV). He doesn't say this out of bitterness, anger, or a dislike for marriage. He actually discusses the beauty of marriage throughout the chapter. His thinking is clearly outlined in the following verses: *"But I want you to be without care. He who is unmarried cares for the things of the Lord, how he may please the Lord."* (1 Cor 7:32 NKJV). I understand this passage to mean there is beauty in marriage and in singleness. At no point does Paul indicate singleness as undesirable or pitiable. There is virtue

in both situations. Singleness can be a time of undivided devotion to God, just as marriage can form good partnerships to perform the work of the LORD.

Additionally, while the Bible is full of examples of godly couples, it is just as full of examples of people recorded as individuals. Jesus himself never married a mortal woman, as the church was to be his Bride. While I would love to get married one day, that may not be God's plan for me. Why would someone want to encourage me to be discontented in my situation when they could instead encourage me to serve the LORD in the way Paul indicates singles can? We should encourage all our acquaintances to be content in whatever situation they are in, as Paul says in Philippians 4:11.

As a single follower of Christ, I do not need a spouse to serve God. I am grafted into Israel's vine, perfectly whole in Christ. Because I'm not yet one flesh with a spouse, I cannot be missing "my other half." My identity is, and always should be, in Christ and the LORD, not in my relationship status. To reduce my persona to merely my romantic relationships ignores my primary identity and purpose.

So, if my objective is to propose a shift in perspective, what changes in thinking do I suggest may be beneficial?

Stop and Take Stock

1. Do not assume those who are single are unhappy. Be one who shows *phileo* love.

2. Before commenting on your single friend's situation, consider whether it will encourage them in their faith journey or rather distract them and cause discontent in their singleness. Additionally, consider what your motivation is for commenting.

3. See single brothers and sisters as valuable members of ecclesial families, not as people to be pitied. Include them, and don't leave them out! I've been excluded from social gatherings because of my singleness, and it feels very isolating.

4. Encourage single brothers and sisters to seek first the Kingdom of God, not relationships. Help them keep their priorities straight.

If we view singleness as a time of happiness and service, perhaps we will be more encouraging to those members who are single. Instead of considering singleness as a lesser state, view it with joy. If the only marriage I ever enter is as the Bride of Christ, I will be perfectly content.

Kate Russell,
(Verdugo Hills Ecclesia, CA)

PRINCIPLES OF COMMUNICATION

By Nancy Brinkerhoff

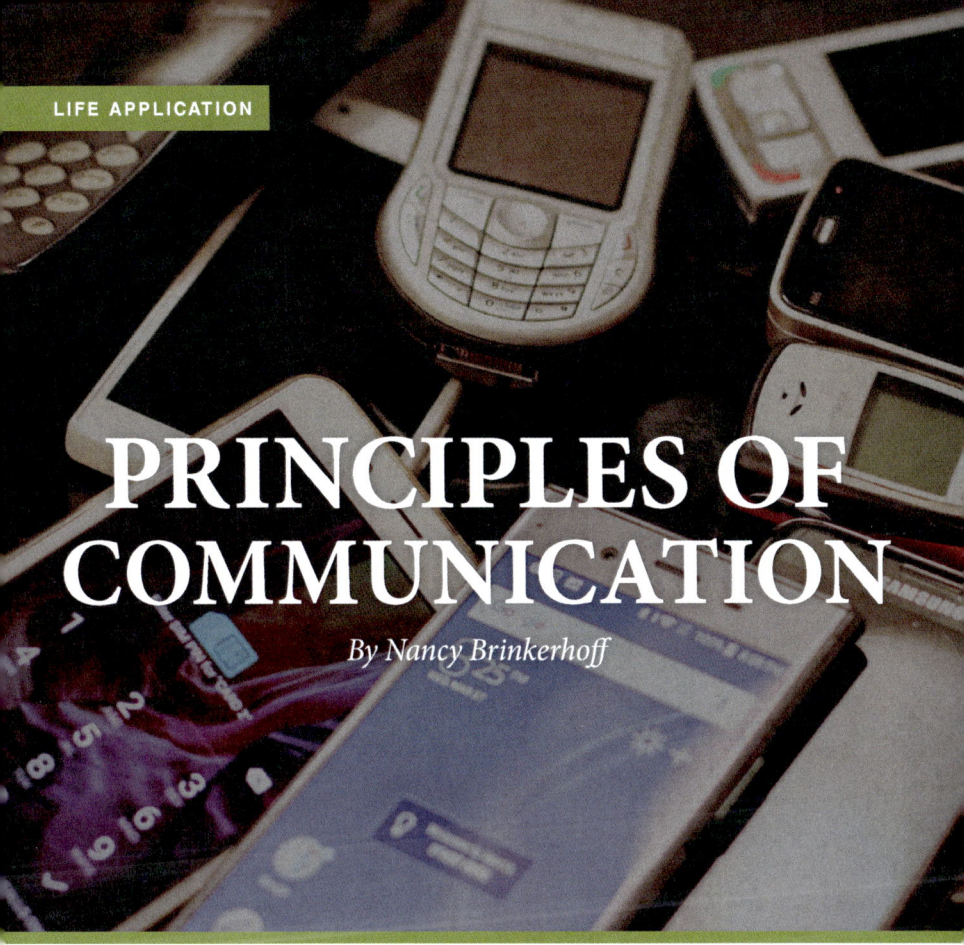

PEOPLE in the 21st century have a dizzying variety of ways to communicate in our global digital age. We place calls on landlines or cell phones. We participate in video calls and virtual meetings. We receive emails, texts, and direct messages on any of a dozen different apps and platforms that we feel compelled to check constantly. We post on various social media sites, then respond to and react to the posts of others. We leave comments, and product reviews scattered far and wide online and interact with other commenters and reviewers. Some of us even enjoy the old-fashioned pleasures of communicating through cards, letters, and visits with friends over coffee.

But it almost goes without saying that this surplus of methods has not necessarily made us better communicators. Mass communication has facilitated gossip and slander and made it much easier to proliferate. Misleading information and outright lies online have become problems for which even national governments can't find solutions. The harsh cruelty of internet comment sections has become legendary. And the subtler sins of pride and envy keep us all presenting an idealized, "curated" version of our lives that leaves everyone less connected and

more unhappy. Far from improving communication, the 21st century keeps creating new terms for all the ways we hurt each other with our words—"trolling," "cyber-bullying," "cancel culture," "man-splaining," "humble-bragging," and "fake news."

Of course, all of this is an old, old story. What may surprise us, however, is to realize how very old a story it is. Modern technology has given us an explosion of new ways to display our selfishness, anger, and pride. But it did not create any of these sins. Thousands of years ago, men and women found ways to cause pain through communication, with no Internet in sight. And perhaps nowhere in the Bible is this more on display than in the Book of Job.

Clearly, the Book of Job is not a treatise on communication. The book leads us through massive theological questions about who God is and how He works in our lives. However, it is also true that most of the text is made up of human beings communicating with each other.

And, mostly, these people do a rather poor job of communicating. Perhaps they had never heard of the term "trolling," but it is easy to spot instances where one of the men in the story makes "an intentionally provocative statement to cause an outsize reaction in a hostile situation." As they grow more and more annoyed at each other for the "patronizing explanations of concepts the listener already knows," modern readers readily recognize "man-splaining."

So, what can 21st century believers learn from the communication missteps of our brethren from thousands of years ago? Quite a lot.

First, it is worth noting that they are consistently described as *"friends."* These men had a history together before the events that caused such antagonism. They are all presented as thinkers and debaters. It is likely that, in happier times they enjoyed getting together for long discussions about points of theology. These friendships were so solid that these men would spend a week of their lives just sitting with Job in his sorrow. However, the dramatic events he experienced were provoking doubts and questions in Job that the others could not cope with. Whatever theoretical or abstract debates they had engaged in before, now things were

> Friendly disagreement gave way to bitter sarcasm and cruel insults.

more real. Friendly disagreement gave way to bitter sarcasm and cruel insults. Though they initially came to comfort Job, all three quickly lost track of that purpose in their drive to prove themselves right and Job wrong.

And it is not at all clear whether their relationship survived the ordeal. Job obeyed the LORD and prayed for his friends at the end of the book. But the men seem to be left out of the final scenes of rejoicing when Job's brothers and sisters, and acquaintances appeared with comfort and gifts. Though they had arrived with good intentions, they allowed angry self-justification to overcome both the reason for their visit and perhaps their whole relationship. If it is true that the harsh debate over

theological differences did destroy these men's friendships, perhaps that is a sad lesson in itself.

It is even more poignant when we remember that both sides of the debate were wrong! They all shared the same unchallenged wrong doctrine of retributive justice. The three friends assumed Job was being punished for a specific sin and insisted–in increasingly spiteful ways–that he repent. Job also assumed such suffering could only stem from major sin and demanded an opportunity to prove his own innocence. Even Elihu, at the end of the debate, took for granted that divine justice on sinners will be evident in this life. In fact, the only one who has next to nothing to say about God's retribution is God Himself.

Perhaps there is a subtle suggestion that, far too often, we humans are arguing about the wrong things. Perhaps, when brothers and sisters debate, both sides are intensely mistaken in their assumptions, so much so that no one in the debate can fully recognize the truth. Perhaps, when we choose sides in these complex questions, we are merely choosing between something deeply flawed and something else even more so. Perhaps one side will eventually deserve three chapters of divine chastisement and repent in dust and ashes, and the other side will need their cowed brethren to make sacrifices for them. At the very least, it should cause us to approach all such disagreements with far more humility. Not that we should give up in our efforts to lead others away from error. But that we should do so with the humble recognition that we ourselves could be wrong in ways we have not yet begun to imagine.

But even those in deep error can raise important and worthwhile points. It is interesting to re-read the early speeches of Job's friends **after** reading about Job's ultimate reward in the epilogue. Many of the exact predictions they made about how God would reward the righteous were fulfilled, some quite precisely. And Eliphaz's instructions to not despise the LORD'S discipline (5:17) are picked up in Proverbs and again in Hebrews. Is it difficult for us to accept that someone we disagree with so profoundly can have something to teach us? Perhaps that is another of the lessons Job and his friends can help us learn about communication.

But, of course, the majority of the words Job's friends say are both wrong and unhelpful. In fact, most of their actual claims are made in Eliphaz's first speech. There are hardly any new arguments in what the other friends say, or in Eliphaz's later words. In fact, the only thing that does change as the speeches continue is the tone.

It does not take long for reason and patience to be replaced by aggression and sarcasm. By the middle of the book, both Job and the friends are beginning each discourse with a few verses of calculated insults before even attempting to make their points. As he starts his second speech, Eliphaz almost seems to realize their discussions are making no headway and perhaps serve no purpose (15:1-3). But then he goes ahead with a full chapter of mostly repeating himself, beginning another round of more of the same.

Why is it that we as humans keep doggedly persisting in an argument, long past the point where it would do any good? Is it a lack of self-awareness– not admitting to ourselves that we have become too annoyed or emotional to have a positive effect? Or is it simply pride, the certainty that I alone have the eloquence that is needed? Whatever the reason, it is tempting to wonder how much better off everyone would have been if Eliphaz had taken his own advice and let go of the argument twenty chapters earlier.

But it is also true that the friends' unhelpful words did provoke Job to learn and grow, though not in the ways they had hoped. After two full rounds of speeches by each of his friends, Job comes to the startling insight that

Job, it should be noted, is the only one in the narrative that does pray.

there have been gaps in his theology. In chapter 21, fully halfway through the book, Job suddenly realizes they have all been wrong. The wicked **do** prosper in this life! (v. 7-26) This is really the only move away from the doctrine of direct retribution in the entire book. Of course, none of the others acknowledge Job's insight, though perhaps the fact their speeches grow noticeably crueler indicates that on some level, they realized he was right.

This is not the only time the friends' words pushed Job in an unintended, yet positive direction. Of the eight speeches Job makes in response to his friends, at least five of them are not directed to the men but to God. The friends' words, unhelpful as they are, prompt Job not just to new realizations but to prayer. Job began the book by praying for his children and ended up praying for his friends. In between, he spent chapter after chapter pouring out to God his sorrow, anger, and hurt. Job's relationship with God shines through on every page. Job, it should be noted, is the only one in the narrative who does pray. How might these discussions have been different if every character in the story talked to God more than they talked to each other?

In summary, the Book of Job stands first as a meditation on theology but also as a profound cautionary tale about human communication. Here are a few of the principles of communication that are illustrated in this strange, thought-provoking narrative. In any situation where communication becomes strained or tense, perhaps Job can lead us to the questions we should be asking ourselves:

1. Purpose—what do I hope to accomplish in the larger context of this relationship?

2. Humility—could I be wrong in how I'm understanding this situation?

3. Openness—is someone making a point I should consider, even if they are wrong in other ways?

4. Self-awareness—am I too annoyed to help or be helped? Should I leave it to another person or another time?

5. Prayer—should I be doing less talking to others and more talking to God?

May God give each of us the grace to learn to communicate better, both with Him and with each other!

Nancy Brinkerhoff,
(Denver Ecclesia, CO)

(With thanks to my teenage daughters, Eve and Prisca Brinkerhoff, for help with this article.)

GOD WILL COMFORT HIS CHILDREN

By Lucas Genner

Bro. Lucas Genner comes from a family of Jewish background which converted to an evangelical church in which he was raised. As he grew up, he was always conscious of his Jewish heritage but felt unsatisfied in his church and was uncomfortable with the idea of a triune God. He tried to connect with Judaism, but after a year of study with an Orthodox congregation and another year with another branch of Judaism, he still felt a lack of spirituality. From both his Jewish and Christian studies, he knew of Jesus as Messiah and began searching the Internet for a non-trinitarian church. He came in contact with the Christadelphians in September 2017, at the age of 22. After going through our correspondence courses with Sis. Jean Hunter, Skype classes with Bro. Andrew Yearsley, and personal Internet classes with Bro. Jim Hunter Lucas was baptized in June 2019 in Córdoba, Argentina by Bro. Rubén Barboza. Bro. Jim and Sis. Jean were in attendance. He continued with Skype classes with Bro. Jim, and through Zoom activities, has gotten to know many of his Latin American brothers and sisters, though still living in isolation in Buenos Aires. Bro. Lucas is a regular contributor of exhortations to the Spanish Christadelphian Isolation League. The following was written for June 26, 2022, and translated by Bro. Dennis Paggi.

IN our reading from the prophet Isaiah, in chapter 51, we find a beautiful message of comfort from God to His people Israel. However, I think these words are apt for us as well since throughout the New Testament, Jesus promises us the same consolation. Paul also teaches us that the followers of Jesus, who are not Israelites, are sons of Abraham through faith (Galatians 3:7) and grafted into the people of Israel (Romans 11). Let's continue now to see this beautiful message from God to all His children.

Isaiah wrote,

> Hearken to me, ye that follow after righteousness, ye that seek the LORD: look unto the rock whence ye were hewn, and to the hole of the pit whence ye were digged. Look unto Abraham your father, and unto Sarah that bare you: for when he was but one I called him, and I blessed him, and made him many. For the LORD hath comforted Zion; and hath comforted all her waste places, and hath made her wilderness like Eden, and her desert like the garden of the LORD: joy and gladness shall be found therein, thanksgiving, and the voice of melody. (Isa 51:1-3).

These beautiful words remind me of the teachings of Jesus on the Mount:

> Blessed are they that hunger and thirst after righteousness; for they shall be filled. Blessed are the pure in heart; for they shall see God. Rejoice and be exceeding glad, for great is your reward in heaven. (Matt 5:6, 8, 12).

Both Isaiah and Jesus emphasized righteousness or justice in their discourses. We understand righteousness in the Bible in two ways. One is the practice of the will of God (in other words, to be righteous). The other is the practice of evaluation and subsequent determination of reward/punishment in a given conflict. Even so, the latter must also submit to the will of God. Our Father tells us that if we practice righteousness and search for it, we will be filled and we will be comforted when the Kingdom is revealed in the earth. Certainly today, most of us do not suffer religious or political persecution for our beliefs like those first followers of Jesus or the prophets of Israel, to whom God said I will do justice for you. However, as children of God, we also need justice and are required to practice it. To love our neighbor as ourselves, to help the needy, and to treat others well and with respect are acts of righteousness we must always undertake. But unfortunately, we often find ourselves with people who are not interested in putting into practice these values and commandments God gives us. So, who has not been mistreated at some point in his life? Who has not been cheated or robbed? Who has not been injured? All of these situations are common, but we, as children of God, cannot get involved in conflicts nor pay back with the same currency as those who cause us harm. Here is where the justice of God enters; we can use it now, as well as in the future. In that case, the Word tells us that all of us who practice righteousness and seek justice will be filled by God on the last day.

Isaiah continues,

> Hearken unto me, ye that know righteousness, the people in whose heart is my law; fear ye not the reproach of men, neither be dismayed at their revilings. For the moth shall eat them up like a garment, and the worm shall eat them like wool: but my righteousness shall be for ever, and my salvation unto all generations. (Isa 51:7-8).

We see we will have the consolation, as part of the promise from God, that all the evil will not touch us, as it does today, and we will fully achieve wellbeing. God will make the wilderness like Eden and give us happiness, joy, and great rewards so that the stress of life will disappear forever. All of us who have the law of God in our hearts are certain this promise will be fulfilled when Jesus returns to the earth. What greater hope can we have than this?

The prophet continues relating the promises of God for those days:

> And the ransomed of the LORD shall return and come with singing unto Zion, and everlasting joy shall be upon their head: they shall obtain gladness and joy: and sorrow and mourning shall flee away. I, even I, am he that comforteth you: who art thou, that thou shouldest be afraid of a man that shall die, and of the son of man which shall be made as grass? (Isa 51:11-12).

These beautiful words are complementary to what is said in Revelation 21:4, "And God shall wipe away all tears from their eyes; and there shall be no more death, neither sorrow, nor crying, neither shall there be any more pain: for the former things are passed away."

God has promised us there will be no more sadness, no more regrets, and no more tribulations in our lives. Our tears will be wiped away by God himself. Therefore, let us not fear man and the damage he can do, for God has promised us better things: righteousness and comfort. Let us know that hope will be fulfilled.

Likewise, the prophet Isaiah continues recounting a great event for Jerusalem. Some will think this occurrence has nothing to do with us today when in fact, it does. As I mentioned at the beginning, we were grafted into the olive tree of Israel, and we are sons of Abraham. While Jerusalem is the capital of the Hebrew nation in the first place, it is also the city God chose for himself (2 Chr 6:6, Psa 132:13). And it is the city of the Great King (Psa 48:2, Matt 5:34-

35). That makes Jerusalem a part of our inheritance. Here the prophet writes,

> Awake, awake, stand up, O Jerusalem, which hast drunk at the hand of the LORD the cup of his fury; thou hast drunken the dregs of the cup of trembling and wrung them out. Therefore hear now this, thou afflicted, and drunken, but not with wine: Thus saith thy Lord the LORD, and thy God that pleadeth

the cause of his people, Behold I have taken out of thine hand the cup of trembling, even the dregs of the cup of my fury; thou shalt no more drink it again. Awake, awake, put on thy strength, O Zion; put on thy beautiful garments, O Jerusalem, the holy city: for hence forth there shall no more come into thee the uncircumcised and the unclean. Shake thyself from the dust; arise and sit down O Jerusalem: loose thyself from the bands of thy neck, O captive daughter of Zion. (Isa 51:17, 21-22; 52:1-2).

God promises to cleanse Jerusalem and make it holy, clean, beautiful, and worthy of the Great King. The name of God will dwell in this city, So we may all climb His mountain and praise him properly. These things allow us to understand how important it is for us to be with Him for eternity. God promised us full consolation and also a dwelling place with Him.

And I John saw the holy city, new Jerusalem, coming down from God out of heaven, prepared as a bride adorned for her husband. And I heard a great voice out of heaven saying, Behold, the tabernacle of God is with men, and he will dwell with them and they shall be his people, and God himself shall be with them, and be their God. (Rev 21:2-3).

And I saw no temple therein: for the Lord God Almighty and the Lamb are the temple of it. And there shall in no wise enter into it anything that defileth, neither whatsoever worketh abomination, or maketh a lie: but only they which are written in the Lamb's book of life. (Rev 21:22, 27).

The new resplendent Jerusalem will be adorned for her husband, Jesus the Lamb, but also for us, children of God, whose names are written in the book of life—the book of the Lamb.

What more could we ask? What more could we hope for? Isaiah, Jesus, and John gave us the best message of hope we can have as children of God. Our Father promised us the salvation of our lives as well as great rewards. To be saved does not just mean being alive or resurrected on that day, but also receiving an incorruptible body and never more experiencing suffering. At that time, *"the wilderness will be made like Eden."* (Isa 51:3). Everything will be happiness, peace, joy, and completeness for each one of us. If we decide to be righteous and seek justice, God has promised to restore the earth that man has destroyed. And He has also promised to restore Jerusalem. This is a special present for all his children: we will enter and dwell together with God and Jesus, who wait for us with their arms open.

Thus, if we desire to have a part in these promises and hopes, if we want to receive this comfort from God, let's answer the call of Jesus in Matthew 4:17, *"Repent ye, for the Kingdom of Heaven is at hand."*

May the peace and blessings of God be with all of you.

Lucas Genner,
(Cordoba, Argentina)

SALVATION IS OF THE LORD!

By Timothy Temilola

SALVATION includes our election, which is past. Our effectual calling and sanctification is the present. And our glorification is what is coming in the future.

We were chosen for salvation by the Father. Jesus Christ redeemed us. The Holy Spirit sanctifies us. God is the author of salvation. His grace is the source from which salvation flows. Jesus is the Savior, and faith is the grace that receives salvation. Separation from the world and dedication to God demonstrates that we are saved, as we manifest the character of our God.

To all this, the Apostle Paul adds, *"We are saved by hope."* (Rom 8:24). Being saved by Hope is not in the same sense as being saved by faith, which can deliver us from guilt, degradation, and eternal death, by receiving and confiding in Christ.

To be saved by Hope is to be sustained in the midst of foes, dangers, and trials. Hope quickens us in duties and prevents us from becoming cold and dead. It comforts us in tribulations and keeps us from being disheartened and gloomy. It enables us to overcome temptation and hold on to our way, looking unto Jesus. It gives us peace in death, in the sure prospect of victory over the grave.

Thus, Hope saves us by preventing despair, into which we can never fall, while Hope lives within us. Hope preserves us from desperation, the verge of which we are sometimes brought. Hope guards us against rebellion, the seeds of which are still thickly sown in our corrupt hearts. Hope protects us from apostasy, into which we can never fall so long as we hope in God. From many evils, at many times, in many ways, we are saved by Hope, sharing in the Hope of Israel, the blessed Hope.

Our Hope is with God as its highest object and best focus. Our Hope is through Christ, who is the way to the Father, the Truth, and the Life. Our Hope is grounded on the Word. Our Hope is for the fulfillment of all God has promised, whether temporal or spiritual, in this world or the next. Our Hope should be encouraged, as it brings glory to God, comfort to our souls, credit to our public profession of faith, and honor to our Lord Jesus Christ.

The Spirit of Truth can fill us with a lively Hope and teach us to expect all God has promised us, all He has revealed in His most holy Word, and all Christ has procured for us.

Timothy Temilola,
(Lagos Ecclesia, Nigeria)

WORDS OF COMFORT, WORDS OF TRUTH

AN INTERVIEW WITH BRO. DAVID SMARTT

By Jessica Gelineau

IN the following conversation, recorded on July 18, 2022, Bro. David Smartt (South Ozone Park, NY) chats with Bro. Levi Gelineau (Simi Hills, CA) about his musical heritage as a Sunday School and CYC student and how these experiences shaped him into someone who now uses original music and lyrics to share the gospel and inspire those around him. The full interview is featured in the Fall 2022 episode of the Good Christadelphian Music podcast, available on whatever platform you use for podcast listening.

Levi: Thanks again for talking with me today, I do really appreciate it. So, tell me more about the music you've done and what you do in your ecclesia, but also the music you produce yourself.

David: Thank you for that question, Levi. At our ecclesia, we usually sing traditional hymns on Sunday mornings for the Memorial Service. In the afternoon, when we have a praise and worship session, we usually sing songs from our Praise the Lord book. The atmosphere is more relaxed, and this is when we incorporate musical instruments. As I matured over the years, I better understood it's not about

CYC and Sunday School students sing songs at a local nursing home during the holiday season.

the instruments and how they make you feel, but it's about the words we sing and how they inspire.

As we get older, we actually start to listen to the words of the hymns and the words of the songbook because when we're younger, those songs and words don't resonate. We haven't yet experienced life. But as we get older, we start to find comfort in the words. And that's what I do with my music. During the pandemic, everyone was inside, and no one was able to come outside. I couldn't even go outside for a run. The things we normally do, we were unable to do. So, where can we find comfort? So how do to find escape?

Music is a way for me to put my mind on the page, but also for using the gospel in a way that allows the Word to be preached. Perhaps not in a traditional way, per se, because I rap, I sing. So, I just put those words of comfort into the songs. When people hear them, they hopefully say, "I needed this." It may be a brother or sister in isolation. Maybe they needed those words for their peace of mind? They may have needed to hear a fellow brother or sister say those words. It's the journey, like the song that I wrote called "It's

the Journey." It says, "Sometimes you lose your way, but God knows you'll be okay." Everyone's on their own journey. Everyone's on their own path. So that's the reason why I make my music. It talks a little bit about my life experiences. The Bible says, *"Be transformed by renewing of your mind."* (Rom 12:2). This includes how we look at everything in life. I try to put that into the songs so people can feel better about themselves and process things.

Levi: What's music like for your ecclesia?

David: Well, I'm at South Ozone Park Ecclesia in Queens, New York. With Bro. Philip [Hinds] playing the piano,

Bro. David at the South Ozone Park Ecclesial Hall

the music is magical! But during the pandemic, we had to switch to using the WCF Hymns for Sunday.[1] Thank God we had those hymns that we were able to rely on. They've been a huge part of our switch to the online platform. It's just a different experience. I hope we get back to having the piano and the in-person fellowship a lot more so we can grow in that aspect.

Levi: Sometimes I feel like it's hard to even remember a time before the pandemic, but what was music like for you guys then? Did you have music events? Did you guys have a choir or something?

David: Oh yeah. We had a choir before the pandemic. It's more of a "You've got to be there" type of experience. And I find the practices are a lot more fun than the performance.

We would practice for an hour, and just joke around for seven hours. There was some important bonding that occurred during this period. I'm the youth leader now for our CYC. So, I invited a few brothers and sisters who live in different countries or some who have not been motivated to come to the ecclesia. They weren't participating much anymore. And now they're all speaking at the CYC, and we have no idea how much that meant to that brother or sister for us to reach out to them. Some responded when asked to talk to the kids by saying, "Of course, I was waiting for you guys to ask me!" Every time we did a concert, it was amazing. We never had a miss of a concert. It was always a hit, always. Those experiences played a huge role in who I am now.

> We haven't yet experienced life. But as we get older, we start to find comfort in the words. And that's what I do with my music.

Levi: The practices for the concerts are better than the actual performance?

David: My Pops (Bro. Tyrone Smartt) was the one who started the CYC in our ecclesia. Sis. Janelle Valz and I were just talking about this while we were in the Philippines. My father used to pick up the CYC members, twenty of them, in a small van! He took all of us to CYC every single week. Sometimes we would all stay at the ecclesia until three, sometimes four in the morning.

A Praise and Worship night at the 2009 Guyana Youth Conference

Bros. Philip Hinds, David Smartt and Paul Hinds at a community outreach event.

Levi: You're doing your own performances, right?

David: Sometimes I go out to 42nd street (NYC), and I perform out there. I emcee, I host, and I DJ sometimes. But that was because I was put on stage from a young age. Growing up in our neighborhood was kind of tough, but the music was an outlet. It was a way for us to be ourselves and a way for us actually to grow in the Spirit and in the faith. We didn't see it then. But of course, kids don't see it until they get to a certain age where they can appreciate it.

Levi: Have you ever felt that the music you do, being different from traditional Christadelphian music, is a challenge for you at all? Have you ever thought of it?

David: No, not really. I wouldn't say that because it's about the words. It's really about the words. I don't curse. I try my best to ensure the lyrics are Scriptural or positive.

Levi: What about inspiration? When you're writing your own stuff, what inspires you? How does that happen? Try to explain that to someone who's never done that themselves. Tracks like "Hostile Takeover" and "The More I See." You wrote those tracks. Please explain the motivation to do that, because I think for a lot of people that doesn't come naturally, right?

David: Well, the motivation, mainly, was to preach. The Bible says, *"Go into all the world and preach the gospel."* (Mark 16:15). So that was my form and way of preaching. My music is a piece of me, meaning my culture, New York's culture. It's all mixed into one. You'll hear all of it. When people listen, they know when it's genuine and when it's from the heart. Whatever you put into your song, the feelings, the emotions, people feel those exact feelings and emotions. So, the motivation is to

really go out there and see who needs help. People are not going to like what we preach. People are not going to like what we say, just as they were with Jesus.

When we go out there and just speak our truth, I definitely believe what we believe Scripturally. I'll give you a little piece of it, and you could take it how you want, you know? We are told that if the people in that place don't want to listen, dust your feet off, and keep moving. (Matt 10:14). So, with the tracks being on Spotify, if the people are searching for that music, that's

Bro. David singing to the newly wedded couple, Bro. Reymon and Sis. Lovely.

something they sought out because they like something about me. They want to hear something. Why do they come back to my page? Obviously, they got something; it's not hurting them. You try to find something that is helping in some way.

Levi: Alright, let's switch gears a little bit. You went to the Philippines on a trip with WCF a couple of months ago.

What was that like?

David: Well, it was a 20-hour flight, which was surprisingly not that bad. I was there with Bro. Daniel Madray and Sis. Janet Link and it was great, as we kept each other company. The hospitality was amazing. And you can sense the unity within the brothers and sisters in the ecclesia. It's like a close-knit family.

We tried to fit in where we could. Daniel and I found a place with the audio; we always tried to help out. I think that's the cool thing about Christadelphians worldwide. It's always, how can I help? And we had an amazing surprise wedding that we were all randomly invited to. In the US, that just doesn't happen. I ended up singing for the wedding, and that was amazing. I wrote a wedding song called "Look in my Eyes," and they allowed me to perform it there.

Levi: Thank you for your time. This has been great.

To listen to David's songs, Search "DavidSmarttMusic" on YouTube or "David Smartt" on Spotify or wherever you stream music. Look for his newest song, "It's the Journey," on Instagram: @ DavidSmarttMusic. Bro. David Smartt can be contacted at asmarttslife@ gmail.com.

We thank him again for taking the time to share his experiences and thoughts!

Jessica Gelineau,
(Simi Hills Ecclesia, CA)

---

[1] Williamsburg Christadelphian Foundation Hymns for Sunday Directory:https://www.wcfoundation. org/hymns

JOSEPH: WE ARE ALL TRUE MEN

By James McCann

THERE are many faithful family legacies in the Bible. In our first article, we looked at the amazing Abraham, who *"lifted up"* his eyes to see Christ's day. In this second article, we are going to look at how Joseph began a legacy that had an eternal impact, not only on the people of his day but for generations to come.

As with all faithful legacies, they will converge on the greatest of all, our Lord Jesus Christ. This is particularly true of Joseph, who is noted as one of the greatest types of Christ in all of the Bible. In fact, the Divine intention of connecting Joseph to Christ in this section of Genesis can be observed right from his very introduction into the record.

Note the inspired contrast between the *"generations of Esau"* in Genesis 36:1 to *"the generations of Jacob"* in 37:1-2. The former is a list of Esau's offspring, which would be expected to follow such an introduction. A list of all the great men of the world, full of fleshly pride, fitting of the many which make up *"the seed of the serpent."*

Now see the contrast to the promised seed of Jacob. *"Joseph being now seventeen years old."* (Gen 37:2). No long list, rather a single focus on just ONE person. There is only one *"seed of the woman,"* that is Christ (Gen

3:15). All those who will make up the multitudinous Christ will be *"in him,"* for there is no other name under heaven in which we can be saved.

We could immediately follow the amazing parallels between Joseph and Christ. From him being beloved of his father, his shepherding of his brothers, his wrongful treatment, his condemnation then exaltation, to finally becoming the savior of the world. Yet there is one aspect that we want to focus on in this consideration of Joseph. It is his role as prophet and priest and the impact on making his brothers into *"true men."*

We can see in the record how Joseph was called to be a prophet and priest to his brothers, not only in the coat that Jacob gave him but in the dreams God divinely revealed to him. Note how the number two occurs in Joseph's life as a key: two dreams shared with family (Gen 37), *"Yahweh was with Joseph"* (39:2-3), *"made him prosper"* (39:2-3), *"Yahweh was with Joseph"* (Gen 39:21, 23), *"in Joseph's hand"* (39:22-23), two servants and another two dreams (Gen 40), *"after two years"* (Gen 41:1), another two dreams to Pharaoh (Gen 41), *"God has showed Pharaoh what He is about to do"* (Gen 41:25-28), two trips to Egypt (Gen 42, 43), *"bowed themselves"* (Gen 43:26, 28). The reason for this significance is explained by Joseph: *"the doubling of Pharaoh's dreams means that the thing is fixed by God, and God will shortly bring it to pass."* (Gen 41:32). Joseph knew the power of God working in his life, even from the age of seventeen, and stepped up to the role of prophet and priest!

The importance of this is found in another Divine contrast in the record. Right in the middle of Joseph's life is Genesis 38 and the dark record of Judah's transgressions. This is even over and above the sin of the brothers recorded in the latter half of Genesis 37, where they sold their brother into slavery. So why is this recorded for us?

There is an inspired play in the Hebrew words found in Genesis 37:32-33 that occurs again in Genesis 38:25-26, helping us draw out the connection's purpose.

As the brothers came to their father, they say; *"This have we found: know now if it be thy son's coat."* (Gen 37:32). The word *"know"* is *"na-kar,"* meaning to scrutinize the evidence, but here it is in the present tense. Then it says: *"Their father knew it."* (Gen 37:33). The word *"knew"* is *"na-kar"* again, but this time in the past tense.

The same sequence and play on words occur with Judah. *"Discern I pray thee, whose are these, the signet."* (Gen 38:25). The word *"discern"* is *"na-kar"* in the present tense. Then it says that *"Judah acknowledged it."* (Gen 38:26). This is the word *"na-kar"* in the past tense!

This is not just showing they are dishonest men, but how God was working to turn their folly back upon themselves! These were men who would use evidence or any means necessary to justify their position, rather than admit their untruthfulness. These were men who were of the promised seed, called to be the family of God on the earth,

> ## "How vital it is that our private life, family life, work life and especially ecclesial life reflects truth, God's truth!"

yet there was not a shred of truth in them. The relevance to us is powerful! We can be part of the ecclesia, part of "The Truth," yet not allow God's truth to renovate our hearts and minds.

The record of Jacob's family is not here just to show us how dysfunctional family life can become, but so we ensure that our lives are *"full of grace and truth."* How vital it is that our private life, family life, work life, and especially ecclesial life reflects truth, God's truth! This is not just a set of doctrines but also a way of speaking, acting, and dealing with others. Let us not be found thinking we can weaponize our faith (like Levi and Simeon in Gen 34) or deal underhandedly to make the end justify the means. This was not Joseph. But it was his brothers, and Joseph wanted to turn them back to being *"true men."*

The impact of the treachery against Judah in Genesis 38 was the first time that Judah saw the treachery of his ways, and it began to impact him. We can trace his conversion and his

brothers as we follow them down into Egypt in Genesis 42. God had forced their hand, and now they stood before the Governor of Egypt. Yet note what it says of Joseph in Genesis 42:6-7. The word *"na-kar"* is used four times, whereas the second time is used as Joseph *"made himself strange to his brothers."* But they *"knew him not"*! How their position had reversed since their deception of their father.

Joseph's desire to turn them back to God is immediately recorded for us in Genesis 42:9. In remembering the dreams, he was about to act in a way that may have looked like revenge, but nothing could be further from the truth. This was of God, and Joseph wanted to draw them back to Him. Like Christ to Peter in John 21, or Christ to Israel in the future (Zech 12), it was going to take a skillful shepherd to bring them to acknowledge their past treachery and to renew a right spirit in their lives. God wants *"truth in the inward parts"* (Psalm 51:6), and Joseph was going to teach them this.

His motivation is clearly demonstrated in Genesis 45.

Joseph immediately challenges them and brings them to trial. Joseph's charge, *"You are spies,"* was a just claim based on their past. One who hides their true motive, who slanders and speaks falsely to cover their tracks. So how would they react? What was now in the hearts and minds of these men who he had seen act so treacherously in the past?

This time, they were forced to examine themselves and answer, *"We are true men."* But were they? Had their attitude changed? As they were pressed, they are forced to speak about their family and, for the first time that they are *"twelve brethren"* of which *"one is not."* They had now acknowledged the one they had once hated. But what did they feel about him and what had happened?

Joseph set out to find out their hearts and minds through a carefully constructed trial. *"Hereby you shall be proved..."* (42:15), *"That your words may be proved, whether there is truth in you."* (v. 16), *"This do and live, for I fear God"* (v. 18), *"If you are true men"* (v.

19), *"So shall your words be verified."* (v. 20). You can see the focus of Joseph in these words about truth.

All that now befell them should have made them think of the past. The brothers, once angered by his dreams (Gen 37:20), had sold him for profit (37:28), mistreated their younger brother (37:23-24), mocked the *"dreamer,"* (37:19), cast him in a pit (37:24), and made up evidence to condemn him (37:31-32). Now Joseph, upon remembering the dreams (42:9) put money in their sacks, sat them in age order of brothers, called himself the *"diviner"* (of dreams), cast Simeon into prison, and made up evidence to accuse them. But Joseph's ultimate test was to bind up their lives in their youngest brother (42:20). How would they NOW respond to this?

The emotion of this record is brought out as the brothers DID begin to reflect on the past. Genesis 42:21-24 shows us their genuine self-examination and sorrow of heart. They who had *"not heard"* (used twice) their little brother's cries now saw the anguish of their brother Simeon (which means

"hearing") taken and cast into prison. During all this, it was Judah who first showed Godly repentance. Contrasting Genesis 42, when they returned to Jacob, in Genesis 43, we see it is Judah who takes the lead, stands up, and speaks (43:3, 8). Furthermore, it was Judah who was willing to give his OWN life for the life of his youngest brother (43:8-9). Then in Egypt, it was again Judah who demonstrates a love for his father and brothers and, in truth declares this to Joseph, even willingly humble about his father's love of Benjamin (Gen 44:14-34). How much he had changed! From not wanting *"his hand to be upon"* Joseph as justification for the deception (Gen 37:27), to now where he becomes surety for Benjamin, *"of my hand you shalt require him"* (Gen 43:9), we see Judah's amazing conversion.

Yet Joseph's last tests were to be the most powerful. First, the open and obvious favoritism of Benjamin in front of them all (Gen 43:34), then tricking and fraudulently charging them as thieves (Gen 44:1-6). How close to home these were! Judah had been the leader in the original deception, then himself deceived. His legalism, which sold his father a lie, was the same that exposed him. Joseph's tests had brought them to the very truth that exposed them!

Judah's reply is so moving that even Joseph is brought to tears (Gen 43:16-34). What true and heartfelt appeal was seen in Judah. What love and compassion he showed towards his father and brothers. What acknowledgment of their wrong and treachery he admitted. Such a picture of the future response of Israel to Christ (Zech 12:10-14, Jer 50:4-6, Acts 2:36-40). Such should be our response to Christ who has made us *"true men."*

This is the legacy of Joseph. Israel was to be reminded of this in years to come. When Joseph's bones were faithfully carried out of Egypt and buried in Shechem (Josh 24:32), it was here that Joshua gathered the people to teach them that they could only serve God *"in sincerity and truth."* (Josh 24:14). Sincerity relates to the genuine and complete integrity that our life must be in service to God. Truth must be more than just a set of doctrines; it must be the truthful hearts and minds seen in our actions and words.

Jesus himself was at Shechem in John 4, near the parcel of ground given to Joseph, when he also drew on this legacy. The powerful message was the same. Those that worship God *"must worship Him in spirit and truth."* (John 4:24). It was the woman of Samaria who *"truly"* (4:18) confessed her life and came to acknowledge her need for the living water that came from Christ *"the saviour of the world."* May we, like her, become part of Joseph's *"fruitful bough by a well, whose daughters run over the wall."* (Gen 49:22). May we be *"true men"* in every aspect of our life, worshiping God *"in spirit and in truth."*

James McCann,
(Riverwood Ecclesia, Australia)

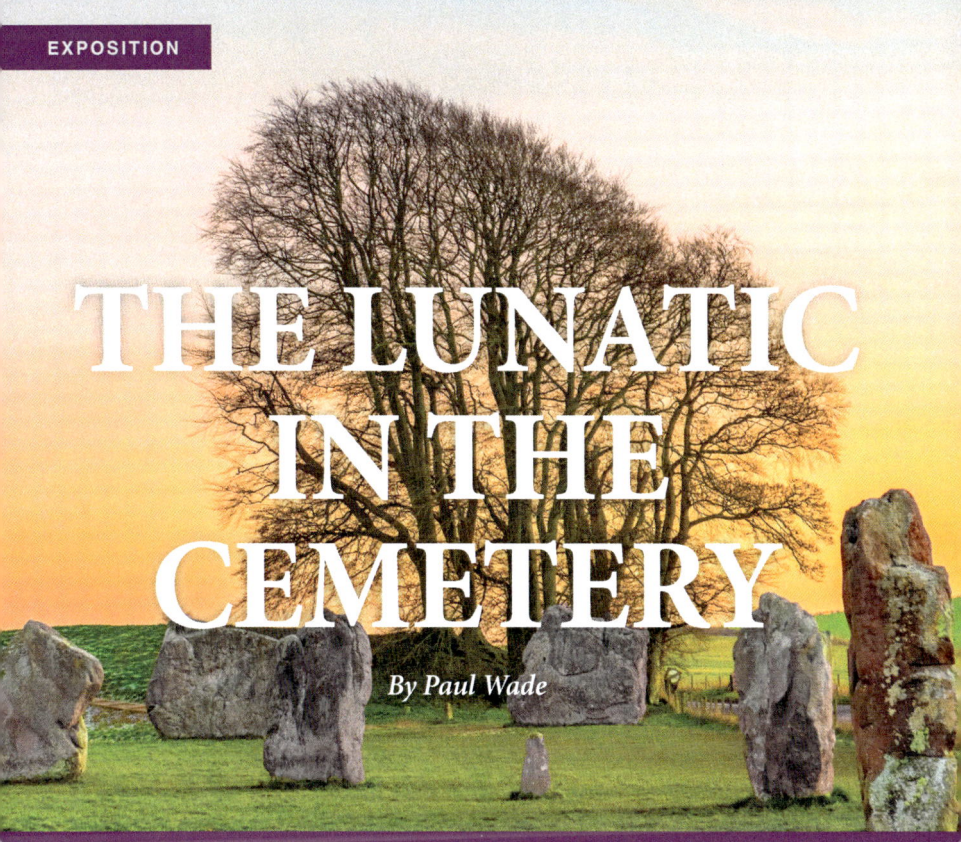

THE LUNATIC IN THE CEMETERY

By Paul Wade

ONE of the most important aspects of reading and studying the Bible is to read carefully, trying in our minds to picture exactly what is meant, what is taking place, and where it is happening. In doing this, we get a far greater lesson from God's Word than we might if we casually read it. This is often called "reading between the lines." In other words, we must use our imagination to try to discover the hidden meaning, and sometimes this involves a bit of speculation. This speculation allows us to come to conclusions that may or may not be fully accurate. Our goal will be that at least they can be good and logical assumptions based on what we know from the Scriptures.

The story for this article is the lunatic in the cemetery. It is one of the most horrifying stories in all the gospel record. The first question we might ask is, "Why is this story here?" We can be certain it is there for a reason, so let's now try to identify the purpose.

We find the account in Mark 5:1-20, Matthew 8:28-34, and Luke 8:26-39; however, we will mostly stay focused on Mark for this article.

The first thing to determine is where this event took place. In both Mark and Luke, it is called *"the country of the Gadarenes."* However, in Matthew, it is called *"the country of the Gergesenes."* The area of Gergesa is also known as

Gerasa. It is the only place that fits the description of the three gospel accounts. This city is on the northeast shore of the Sea of Galilee.

Today there is a Jewish kibbutz at this location, known as Ein Gev. When I visited this kibbutz, residents told me this was the site where Jesus healed the lunatic. Indeed, there is a hill there with a steep incline, where it is possible the swine could have rushed into the Sea of Galilee and drowned.

After crossing the Sea of Galilee by ship, Jesus arrived at the area of Gergesa, and immediately a man ran toward him. This was no ordinary man. He was insane, a lunatic, demon-possessed, or with an unclean spirit in the language of the day.

The record states, *"He had his dwelling among the tombs."* (Mark 5:3). The Revised Version is more accurate when it says, *"He had his dwelling In the tombs."* Therefore, he lived in caves with stones in front of most of them. Perhaps he stayed in a different cave each night, sleeping among the dead bodies.

The next thing stated is that *"no man could bind him, no, not with chains."* (v. 3). Why? Because he broke both the fetters and chains that bound him. Fetters are shackles. So he was bound hand and foot. But even then, he could break these bindings with his enormous strength. Most likely, he was a severely injured man, with blood running down his arms and legs. Another thing to ponder is how did they get these chains and fetters on him in the first place? We were told no man could bind him, so we might assume they must have knocked him out to accomplish this.

He must have been in excruciating pain. No wonder it says, *"Night and day, he was in the mountains, and in the tombs, crying, and cutting himself with stones."* (v. 5). Surely, he was in extreme agony, with his body covered by injuries and infection. Remember, he dwelt with dead bodies. In other words, he was dead while he lived. When we read an account like this, we rarely take time to imagine the scene fully. To make it worse, he was naked. Just how do you think he smelled?

When he sees Jesus, he runs and falls at his feet, saying, *"What have I to do with thee, Jesus, thou Son of the most high God? I adjure thee by God, that thou torment me not."* (v. 7).

There are two items of importance expressed here. The first is an acknowledgment that Jesus was the Son of God. To know this, he must have overheard talk among the people around Gergesa. Few of them believed it; however, this insane man did. The second point is his statement, *"I adjure thee by God."* Where have we heard that phrase before?

> And the high priest arose, and said unto him, Answerest thou nothing? What is it which these witness against thee? But Jesus held his peace, And the high priest answered and said unto him, I adjure thee by the living God, that thou tell us whether thou be the Christ, the Son of God. (Matt 26:62-63).

It was as if this insane man were prophesying what the High Priest would say at the trial of Jesus.

Jesus then heals the man. Why do you suppose, right here at the beginning

God put chains on Israel by His laws and commandments, but Israel could not be bound.

of his ministry, we have this story? Perhaps the answer is given just before this event but in the Matthew account.

And a certain scribe came, and said unto him, Master, I will follow thee whithersoever thou goest. And Jesus saith unto him, The foxes have holes, and the birds of the air have nests; but the Son of man hath not where to lay his head. And another of his disciples said unto him, Lord, suffer me first to go and bury my father. But Jesus said unto him, Follow me; and let the dead bury their dead. (Matt 8:19-22).

Jesus was talking about the sad spiritual condition of the nation of Israel. In Matthew, Jesus referred to the scribes and Pharisees, the religious leaders of Israel, as *"hypocrites." "Woe unto you, scribes and Pharisees, hypocrites! for ye are like unto whited sepulchres, which indeed appear beautiful outward, but are within full of dead men's bones, and of all uncleanness."* (Matt 23:27).

The real reason for this story comes from the Old Testament in the Book of Isaiah.

Ah sinful nation, a people laden with iniquity, a seed of evildoers, children that are corrupters: they have forsaken the LORD, they have provoked the Holy One of Israel unto anger, they are gone away backward. Why should ye be stricken any more? ye will revolt more and more: the whole head

is sick, and the whole heart faint. From the sole of the foot even unto the head there is no soundness in it; but wounds, and bruises, and putrifying sores: they have not been closed, neither bound up, neither mollified with ointment. (Isa 1:4-6).

Do you see in this prophecy the story of the insane man in the cemetery?

1. *"The whole head is sick."* Head wounds from banging his head on the walls within the tombs, from being knocked out so they could apply fetters.

2. *"The whole heart is faint."* The lunatic had lost hope of ever being normal again until he saw Jesus step out of the ship.

3. *"From the sole of the foot even unto the head there is no soundness in it, but wounds, and bruises, and putrifying sores."* Is this not an accurate picture of the bruised and battered body of the insane man?

4. *"They have not been closed, neither bound up, neither mollified with ointment."* Just as nothing had been done to make this man's life any better and no one could treat him, so Israel had done nothing to heal their spiritual wickedness.

This insane man was Israel. The chains were the Law of Moses which Israel had repeatedly broken. God put chains on Israel by His laws and commandments, but Israel could not be bound.

All these chains and fetters were broken repeatedly. The people were crying out to God, but God was not listening because of their wickedness. The lunatic was crying out and cutting himself. Where have we heard this before? Remember the prophets of Baal in the days of Elijah?

And it came to pass at noon, that Elijah mocked them, and said, Cry aloud: for he is a god; either he is talking, or he is pursuing, or he is in a journey, or peradventure he sleepeth, and must be awaked. And they cried aloud, and cut themselves after their manner with knives and lancets, till the blood gushed out upon them. (1 Kgs 18:27-28).

Now, going back to Mark 5, when Jesus healed the insane man, what did he say to him?

For he said unto him, Come out of the man, thou unclean Spirit. And he asked him, What is thy name? And he answered, saying, My name is Legion: for we are many. And he besought him much that he would not send them away out of the country. (Mark 5:8-10).

Even though this sounds simply like dialog between Jesus and the lunatic, look how much of it relates to the nation of Israel's ungodly position. They were unclean spiritually. It was not only a few of them but many. The word *"country"* in verse 10 is the Greek word *"chora,"* which is often translated as land. Once again, let's go back to the prophets.

Then the word of the LORD came unto me, saying, Son of man, they that inhabit those wastes of the land of Israel speak, saying, Abraham was one, and he inherited the land: but we are many; the land is given us for inheritance. (Eze 33:23-24).

This insane man is talking as if he is the fulfillment of this prophecy of Ezekiel. Compare these passages:

Mark 5:9 *"My name is Legion: for we are many."*

Ezekiel 33:24 *"But we are many."*

Mark 5:10 *"And he besought him much that he would not send them away out of the country."*

Ezekiel 33:24 *"The land is given us for an inheritance."*

This is our land, don't send us away out of it. Today, the Tel Aviv Airport has "Erets Israel" written on the entrance wall. This wording means "The land of Israel." What they intend to represent is *"This is our land."* When did we hear these words during Christ's day? *"If we let him thus alone, all men will believe on him: and the Romans shall come and take away both our place and nation."* (John 11:48). The lunatic is representative of Israel in its diseased, insane state.

We should also consider the subject of the pigs. The Jews should not have been tending a herd of swine in the first place. *"Now there was there nigh unto the mountains a great herd of swine feeding. And all the devils besought him, saying, Send us into the swine, that we may enter into them."* (Mark 5:11-12). Perhaps these swine were the lunatic's source of food. If he had eaten the pig's meat, the Jews certainly would have avoided him and considered him unclean.

Let's return to the prophets.

I have spread out my hands all the day unto a rebellious people, which walketh in a way that was not good, after their own thoughts; A people that provoketh me to anger continually to my face; that sacrificeth in gardens, and burneth incense upon altars of brick; Which remain among the graves, and lodge in the monuments, which eat swine's flesh, and broth of abominable things is in their vessels; Which say, Stand by thyself, come not near to me; for I am holier than thou. These are a smoke in my nose, a fire that burneth all the day. (Isa 65:2-5).

Do you think that this is just a coincidence? Look at the similarities in just verses 4-5.

1. *"Which remain among the graves and lodge in the monuments."* That's exactly what Legion was doing, living in the tombs of dead people.

2. *"Which eat swine's flesh"* It seems likely this may have been at least part of his diet.

3. *"Which eat the broth of abominable things."* What could be more abominable than eating human flesh? The lunatic probably did this if he was unable to catch a pig to eat.

4. *"Which say, Stand here by thyself, come not near to me; for I am holier than thou."* (v. 5.) This would certainly be the attitude of the

people of Gergesa. They had tried to subdue him but were unable to.

After Jesus healed the man, the people of the city came out to see what had happened. *"And they come to Jesus, and see him that was possessed with the devil, and had the legion, sitting, and clothed, and in his right mind: and they were afraid."* (Mark 5:15). Rather than seeing a man in a wild frenzy, he was calm and sitting with Jesus. Now he was clothed. You certainly wouldn't clothe someone in his filthy condition without washing him first. This would have been done in the Sea of Galilee, representing baptism. He was now in his *"right mind"* and fully understood that Jesus was the Son of God. He believed in him because he wanted to follow Jesus. Jesus tells him instead to go home and tell his friends about him. That's what we must do too.

What did Legion do to save himself? Nothing. What could he do? What can we do to save ourselves? Nothing. We must believe in Jesus and follow his commandments.

As this pitiful man was healed, so too God will heal the nation of Israel when they turn to Him and follow His commandments, believing that His Son is the true Messiah, Jesus Christ, their Lord.

> We must believe in Jesus and follow his commandments.

Paul Wade,
(Houston West Ecclesia, TX)

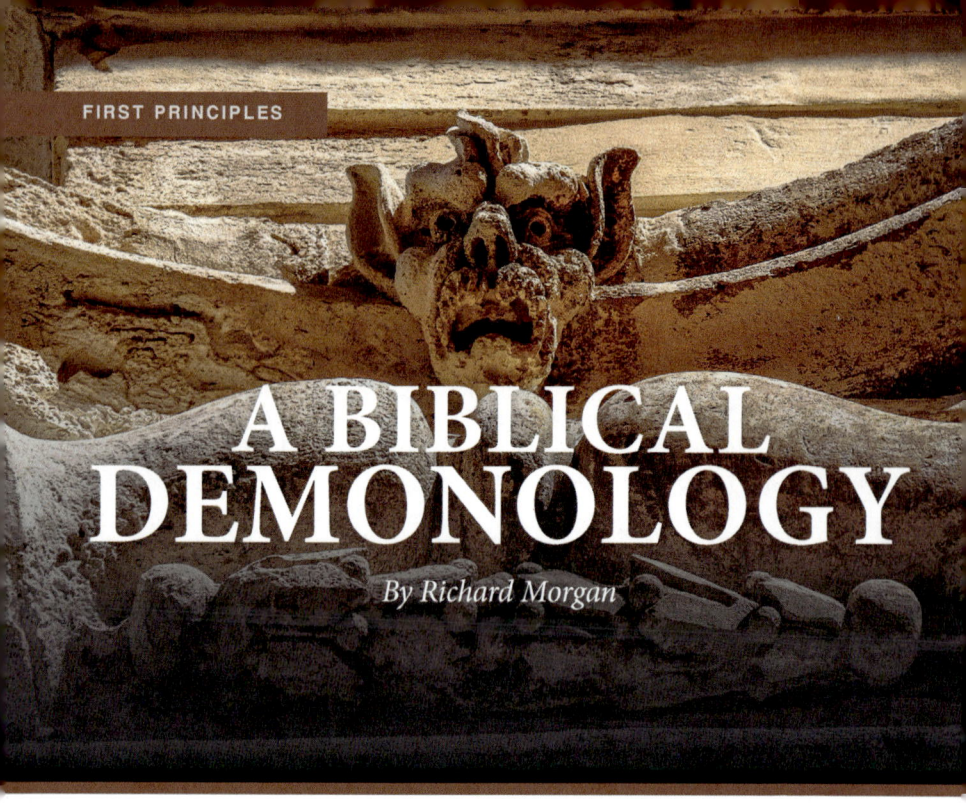

A BIBLICAL DEMONOLOGY

By Richard Morgan

THERE is a tendency among Christadelphians to read the accounts of Jesus casting out demons and assume, "it really means he was curing them of a mental illness." While, from a 21st century perspective, that is probably what happened, it's not a good way to read the Bible. A common term for what we're often guilty of is "demythologizing." On the other hand, the other extreme, "conflict theology," which is common among evangelical expositors, takes the literalist approach to passages about demons and supposes that they represent real supernatural beings in spiritual warfare against God.[1]

The problem with demythologization is we're redefining Bible language using modern-day terms that would have no meaning in the ancient Near East. While we might like to read *"demon-possessed man"* as "man with schizophrenia," that's not what the term means. The Bible translators have done a good job in reflecting the Greek term as *"demon-possessed man,"* and we need to accept that is the case.

However, there is another way to read passages about demon possession that avoids the problem of demythologizing and doesn't go down the route of conflict theology and its inconsistencies with other Bible teachings. That is, to read these passages as *phenomenological*.

The gospel records are eyewitness accounts of the life of Jesus of Nazareth. When Matthew and the other authors (or those apostles that provided details for the gospel writers) saw what Jesus did, they expressed exactly what everyone witnessed—he cast out

What are we to make of the demon miracles, and other occurrences of demons throughout Scripture?

demons. They didn't see Jesus healing someone with a mental illness because that idea had no meaning in the first century. To the onlookers, Jesus did exactly what our English translations record—he cast out demons.

This language is phenomenological in the same way we describe things that we see every day of our lives. We talk about the sun rising in the east because, from our perspective, that's exactly what we see. However, imagine someone two thousand years in the future reading a newspaper article from 2022 where the author states something happened "as they saw the sun rising in the east." Let's suppose that phraseology had died out of usage in the English language, and now cosmic phenomena are defined using strict scientific language. Our hypothetical reader is going to say something like, "what are they talking about? The sun doesn't rise in the east! What utter nonsense—ignorant, primitive people!"

But we have no problem saying the sun rises in the east even though we also understand that it doesn't match our understanding of science that the earth revolves around the sun. We're using phenomenological language because of the phenomenon we observe from our point of view.

Leaving aside whether the gospel writers believed in literal supernatural demons when they penned the gospels, what they wrote about are the phenomena that people witnessed. Jesus cast out demons. That doesn't mean demons have any real existence any more than the sun rises in the east. But what it *does* allow us to do is take the Bible at its word and avoid the logical fallacies we often are guilty of when reading it.

Having said all that, what are we to make of the demon miracles and other occurrences of demons throughout Scripture? The conflict theology approach is to read these passages as theological statements concerning a supposed cosmic war between Yahweh and Satan and his minions. However, in one sense, while accepting the Biblical terms as written, they are committing a similar misreading of the text as the demythologizers by placing meaning on the text that was never intended by the original author—the anachronistic fallacy.

A question we can ask is, were demon passages written to convey theological doctrine? Did the gospel writers, for instance, want their readers to understand something about a cosmic battle when they recorded Jesus casting out demons?

To answer that question, we will start working our way toward Biblical Demonology. We are going to find, after analyzing other Bible texts concerning demons, that the phenomenological language used by the Bible authors is framed within a context that does provide us with insight into theological doctrine but *not* if we go down the route of believing that demons have any real existence.

To aid our study, we will use Paul's speech in Athens as a base. When you read the passage (Acts 17:16-34), you might wonder what any of it has to do with demons because the term, at least in our common English versions, doesn't appear in the text. However, as will become clear, the Greek term *does* appear in the context of Paul's speech. The fact most English translations don't use *"demon"* is probably a testimony that this passage, with its abundant Bible echoes to supporting passages, is key to dismissing the conflict theology argument.

First, a bit of background. Imagine you're Paul, and you've just been tasked with taking the gospel to the Gentiles. You grew up in a Gentile area and know it well. You know, for instance, that the Gentiles are steeped in idolatry. While there may have been acceptance of the existence of Yahweh, he was only a local god for the Jewish people in Judea and one among a multitude of others. How on earth will you convince these people—so strongly superstitiously ruled over by their pagan ideas that there is only one God, and he has a Son? *"And there is salvation in no one else, for there is no other name under heaven given among men by which we must be saved."* (Acts 4:12).

As Paul contemplated his task for the dozen or so years he spent in Tarsus before his first missionary journey, what kind of Bible passages would he consult for guidance? A check of his writings tells us that one of Paul's favorite books was Isaiah. When writing to Gentile ecclesias, such as the ones in Rome and Corinth, he quoted extensively from this book, and especially the so-called "Deutero-Isaiah," chapters 40 through 66. It makes sense for Paul to be keenly interested in those chapters because they address the same problem he would encounter as he preached to the Gentiles. The Jewish nation, as Isaiah records, was going to go into exile, and there in Babylon, they would come face-to-face with the idolatry of the nations. Much of Isaiah's message concerns the conflict between the worldview of the monotheistic Jews and polytheistic Gentiles. Chapters like Isaiah 46 go head-to-head with idolatry and teach the fundamental principle *"I am God, and there is no other."* (Isa. 46:9).

Another of Paul's favorite passages, aside from those in Isaiah, was Deuteronomy 32. He quotes verse 21 of that chapter, for instance, in Romans 10:19, *"I will make you jealous of those who are not a nation; with a foolish nation I will make you angry."* For Paul, taking the gospel to the Gentiles, that

> Imagine you're Paul and you've just been tasked with taking the gospel to the Gentiles.

passage had a lot of meaning. The *"you,"* or the Jewish people, would reject the gospel and the *"foolish nation"* who had once worshiped idols, the Gentiles, would embrace it. Paul's successful mission was prophesied right there in Deuteronomy 32.

Why Deuteronomy 32 in particular? Because it tackles the problem of idolatry head-on, just like in Isaiah. Verse 39 says, *"See now that I, even I, am he, and there is no god besides me,"* phraseology not only found in the passage from Isaiah 46 quoted above but Isaiah 41:4; 43:10-13; 46:4-9, and 48:12-13.

One of the Isaiah passages most associated with Deuteronomy 32 is chapter 44. In Deuteronomy 32:15 and 17 the Hebrew for God is *"eloah,"* an unusual title in contrast with the normal *"elohim."* Isaiah only uses it of God once, in chapter 44:8, *"Is there a God besides me?"*

Also, in Deuteronomy, God is described as a *"rock"* (v. 4, 30-31), and Isaiah follows up his question in verse 8 with the statement, *"There is no Rock; I know not any."*

Perhaps the clearest link between the two passages is Deuteronomy's use of the nickname *"Jeshurun"* (v. 15, also used twice in chapter 33), only found outside of Deuteronomy in Isaiah 44:2. The chapters match each other in their content—the incomparability of Yahweh. Yahweh delivered his people despite their sins as a witness to the nations, and the Gentiles are invited to turn to Yahweh as the only true God. Deuteronomy 32 itself is a hymn, and

in the poetic structure, verse 39 stands out as the only verse in the hymn with a tricola[2], emphasizing its importance:

See now that I, even I, am he,

and there is no god beside me;

I kill and I make alive;

I wound and I heal;

and there is none that can deliver out of my hand.

These words are echoed by Isaiah in the following chapter, 45:5-7:

I am the LORD, and there is no other, besides me there is no God; I equip you, though you do not know me, that people may know, from the rising of the sun and from the west, that there is none besides me; I am the LORD, and there is no other. I form light and create darkness; I make well-being and create calamity; I am the LORD, who does all these things.

It seems clear Isaiah is based on Deuteronomy 32, and Paul understood these passages as they related to his ministry to the Gentiles. Deuteronomy 32, in particular, forms the basis of the theological significance of demons and aids us in our search for a Biblical demonology.

As Acts 17:15 infers, Paul went ahead of his companions to Athens, and he had time to do a bit of sightseeing. Immediately Paul was struck with something that dominated that famous city, *"Now while Paul was waiting for them at Athens, his spirit was provoked within him as he saw that the city was full of idols."* (v. 16).

The phrase *"his spirit was provoked"* echoes with Deuteronomy 32. That chapter warns Israel against embracing the gods of the nations. Verse 16 says, *"They stirred him to jealousy with strange gods,"* and in verse 21, *"they have provoked me to anger with their idols."* Paul, then, has the same emotion as God when seeing a people steeped in idolatry. Wherever you went in Athens, you would see idols. They were in famous public places, like the Acropolis and Agora. Statues of gods and heroes of Greek mythology lined the streets. Athens was also famous for the *Hermae*, which were pillars mounted with the head of Hermes. Athens was a truly polytheistic place, and the Greeks had gods for everything. Apart from the famous Olympian gods like Apollo and Zeus, there were many small gods, as they were termed, like Nyx, goddess of the night, Glaucus, god of the fisherman, and Comus, god of revelry, merrymaking, and festivity. Whatever happened in life, there was a god for it.

Greek culture was steeped in polytheism as a part of their daily lives. "These gods and heroes were not simply up in heaven, enjoying the Muses' gloating over human suffering. Greek life was lived with a sense of their potential presence, in the clamor of storms, or the stresses of sickness, in the dust clouds of battle, or on distant hillsides, especially in the midday sun."[3]

For the Greeks, as with the ancient world in general, the gods existed in everything. Paul's theology, however, as we will come to see, was fundamentally different.

As was Paul's custom, he first found the synagogue and reasoned with the Jews there (v. 17), but his main preaching experience was to be at the Agora, speaking to *"those who happened to be there."* The marketplace (Greek: *agora*) was a famous place in Athens. Apart from being somewhere to buy and sell products, it was a place where Athenians gathered to discuss all kinds of topics like politics and current events.

Luke singles out two groups of Greek philosophers who became Paul's audience, the Epicureans and Stoics (v. 18). It is worthwhile exploring their philosophies since Paul attempts to address both schools of thought in his speech.

In some ways, the different philosophies of the Epicureans and Stoics mirrored the way the Sadducees differed from the Pharisees. The Epicureans, founded by Epicurus in the fourth-century BC, were deists, almost de facto atheists. While they may have believed in the gods, they regarded them as aloof and uninvolved in human affairs. They emphasized pleasure as the main pursuit of human beings, and

so were hedonists as well, although the legend of the pleasure garden of Epicurus is overstated. Epicureanism as a philosophy looked at "questions of perception, ethical aims, and sensations."[4] One of the famous works of Epicureanism was written by the poet Lucretius in the first century BC. Titled *De rerum natura (On the Nature of Things)*, it explored the concept that while the gods may have created the world, that was the limit of their supernatural involvement with mankind.

Anything that happens in this world can instead be explained by natural phenomena, and everything came into being from atoms and particles of matter. They did not believe in divine providence, and the idea of theodicy (an explanation of why evil and God co-exist) was alien to them because the gods simply had no interest in the world. Epicureans also denied any concept of an afterlife, believing that life could not exist outside of the body, and so denied the doctrine of the immortality of the soul. But more importantly, within the context of Paul's speech, they would have difficulty with the concept of the resurrection.

In many ways, the modern-day equivalent of the Epicureans would be those who follow the philosophy of naturalism—the idea or belief that only natural (as opposed to supernatural or spiritual) laws and forces operate in the world, championed by such people as the New Atheists.

The Stoics swung towards the opposite extreme of the spiritual pendulum, emphasizing belief in the gods. They had a theology more in line with general thought in the ancient world, that divinity was found in everything. This belief, also called pantheism, meant that the concept of a delineation between the natural and supernatural was meaningless; everything had a supernatural explanation. It was the Stoic philosophy that Paul was more concerned with. He even quoted Stoic philosophers in his speech to prove his point. However, what he is inviting the Stoics to do is have a paradigm shift in their understanding of the supernatural. He is trying to turn the philosophical world upside-down. Paul was not a pantheist, and he demonstrates the sovereignty of Yahweh, God of Israel, instead as a distinct contrast with the concept of the godhead in the ancient world.

Richard Morgan,
(Simi Hills Ecclesia, CA)

*Lord willing, this series will continue with **Part 2** in the next issue.*

---

[1] For more details on demythologizing and conflict theology, see Walton, John H., and J. Harvey Walton. *Demons and Spirits in Biblical Theology*. Cascade Books, 2019.

[2] A tricola is a rhetorical term used in poetry for a series of three parallel clauses. See Labuschagne C. (2013). *The Song of Moses in Deuteronomy 32—Logotechnical Analysis.*

[3] Fox R.L. (2005). *The Classical World an Epic History of Greece and Rome.* Penguin Books. p52.

[4] Ibid. p273.

ROBERT ROBERTS IN NORTH AMERICA

(PART 2)

By Peter Hemingray

Bro. Peter Hemingray's article continues, picking up in January 1889, with the "Sugar Disaster" unfolding.

IT is not the place here to describe details of one of the greatest frauds of the 19th century, which unfortunately greatly affected many Christadelphians. It is covered widely on the Internet.[1] The disappointing results are described in *The Christadelphian*:

> On the morning of Thursday, January 3rd, 1889, I received

a cable-message from brother James U. Robertson, of New York, which for a season hurled me into darkness. It was an intimation that a discovery of a 'terrible' character had just been made in reference to the sugar refining enterprise, which he had been nursing for four years. The message did not say what the discovery was, but added that there was no doubt of its truth. The message affected me more than any I have received in the course of my life. Every form of prosperity for the work of God upon earth was bound up in the success of that enterprise. The Jewish colonization of the Holy Land was to be helped as no Gentile, and no Jew after the flesh either feels moved to help it. The truth was to be published, both by lecture and literature, as it has never been in this generation. The poor were to be helped as never in our age has been possible. Every grievous load among the brethren, under which private hearts are bleeding, was to be undone. An institution for the annual recuperation of the ailing by a three weeks' free stay, to which railway fare would be paid to and fro, was to be provided. Other forms of service, not as yet so distinctly defined, were to be entered upon.[2]

No one thought Robert Roberts was looking for personal gain but only for help for the Jews and the gospel.

As soon as he got the cable, he and his wife set out for New York, arriving only to confirm the venture's complete collapse. They had departed immediately after receiving the cable and, after several misadventures, caught a steamer from Ireland, arriving in New York on Wednesday, January 16. They departed on Saturday. There were numerous ramifications, but this is not the place to discuss them.

1889 August

This visit was noted almost in passing in *The Christadelphian*, in the notes for September 1889, where we read,

THE EDITOR'S VISIT TO THE STATES—From this the Editor safely returned on Sunday, August 25th, his journey to the States has been sufficient of a success to justify the hope (not yet amounting to certainty) that the losses caused to the brethren by the sugar imposture will ultimately be made good.

We know a little more from *The Advocate*, for at the time, Roberts had good relations with the editor, Thomas Williams, and they were together again at the annual gathering in Wauconda. Much later, it was reported that Williams and Roberts met together in harmony, but this was soon to be disrupted, mainly by J. J. Andrews, but that is another story.

It was on the beautiful lake that skirted the homestead that Thos. Williams and Robert Roberts, seated in a small boat, Roberts in the stern and Williams rowing over its waters the day after the gathering, for three hours discussed the responsibility question in all its bearings and arrived at a good working basis of cooperation.[3]

Robert Roberts disputed this cooperation later when he said, "the result of the conversation was… doubtful."[4] It was also noted that Roberts was in business with James Robertson, whom

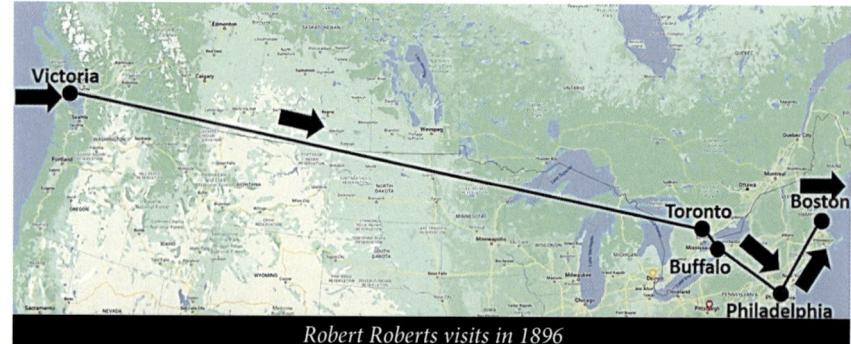
Robert Roberts visits in 1896

he met after the gathering in Chicago, and returned to Wauconda to conduct business there, clearly hoping to recoup from his Sugar Disaster.

Unfortunately, the Sugar Disaster was only the start of a series of misadventures he embarked upon, all of which were disastrous and affected his health so gravely that he was advised to take a sea voyage. Others encouraged him to remove himself from such further efforts. So, he decided to accept an invitation and go to Australia, leaving in late August 1895.

1896 Back from Australia

Originally scheduled to leave Australia on May 18, he did not leave until June 10, 1896, so his schedule in North America was somewhat pruned. The uncertainty of his actual arrival date caused a rather amusing episode on his arrival in Victoria, B.C. He was summarily deposited on the quay at 4 a.m., eventually arriving at the house of his host, Thomas Edwards, at 7 a.m. He left his considerable luggage on the doorstep and went for a walk, only to be accosted a little later by his host, somewhat timidly.

This late arrival also caused some modifications to his itinerary, so he only visited the above ecclesias. Of course, it was all just a minor part of his journey back to England, arriving back in England on August 16, having spent two years away from his family.

Victoria. He spent about 11 days in the city, lecturing many times. The ecclesia at the time numbered about twenty as a result of some turmoil caused by recent dissident arrivals from Scotland. But there was some good news: a year later, a correspondent reported he had been baptized after picking a flyer up from the street and attending the lectures.

The "comparatively invalid" set out on the recently completed Canadian transcontinental railroad for five days and nights to Ontario. Changing in North Bay, it was a mere nine hours to Toronto, where he had been a few years before.

Toronto. Roberts only spent two days there, and no public lectures had been planned, so it was mostly a time for friendly visits. Edwin Hill was his host, who later played a prominent part in Conscientious Objection during WW1. The ecclesial situation in Toronto was complex. There were three ecclesias, one "Central" reported by William Smallwood, which Roberts visited, and others of the *Fraternal Visitor* and *Advocate* fellowships. Roberts attempted to unite the first two but with no lasting results. On the other hand, he had a much more pleasant visit to Buffalo.

Buffalo. Arriving on Friday, July 24, he stayed until the following Thursday, delivering about six lectures and enjoying his time there. Here he again stayed with Bro Stricker. The news in *The Christadelphian* later said several were still attending after his lectures, so at least a few responded to his message. He left on Thursday for a lightning visit to Philadelphia, about five hundred miles away, taking 12 hours through pleasant countryside.

Philadelphia. This ecclesia was where James Robertson had settled, but not without attempting further ill-considered ventures, for he was suffering from "failure of business hopes." He met with the ecclesia (of about 30) on Friday evening and on

Saturday morning, left for the 300-mile trip to Boston, passing through New York City without stopping due to his appointment in Boston on Saturday night.

Boston. Last stop on his journey: he delivered several lectures during his stay for the week: once such "Preparing for Armageddon" was the subject of a report in the next morning's paper, and as Roberts said, "The notice was more accurate than usual." To quote:

> He (Robert Roberts) is a short, thickset man physically, with a large head and a conspicuous face. He has a habit of turning his eyes upward when he's about making any particularly obscure sentence, and when his statement is likely to be received with doubt he emphatically asserts that there can be no question about it... Mr. Roberts did not make any statement as to the date of Christ's coming, but he was certain that the visible Christ would come soon, for the disturbed state of the world proved it.[5]

There were about 150 present at the Memorial service on Sunday, including some from the nearby region, so Boston was still probably the largest ecclesia in North America. Roberts also intervened with about fifteen members who were separated over erroneous ideas about the unpardonable sin. It was later reported that his efforts were successful. He also attended a social gathering, but under challenging circumstances—a relatively small apartment on a busy street with closed windows, with six

The community had grown from about 1,000 at the time he launched *The Christadelphian* magazine to over 10,000 when he died.

fainting in the heat. But he struggled on. He left for England after a stay of five days.

Conclusion

Robert Roberts arrived back in England on Saturday, August 16, for a welcome reunion with his wife. He stayed there for almost a year, leaving with his family (less son) for Australia on August 2 next year, planning to remain in Australia but with periodic visits back to England. According to this plan, he left Australia on August 2, 1898, and landed in San Francisco on his way to Victoria on the morning of Sept 21.

He was only fifty-nine when he died, but he had been unwell for some time, burdened by financial catastrophe, efforts for the Truth when ill, as well as the recent news his only son, Edward Augustus, had left the community. He had given structure and vigor to the Christadelphians, traveling much of the world to spread the message from 1864 on. The community had grown from about 1,000 at the time he launched *The Christadelphian* magazine to over 10,000 when he died. The community might have been somewhat divided, but all acknowledged his considerable contributions, and messages of grief poured in from all quarters.

And we in North America will be eternally grateful for his work on these shores.[6]

Peter Hemingray,
(Pittsburgh Ecclesia, PA)

[1] This episode had many ramifications, including in Milan, MI: a few from that town were sentenced to prison in late 1889. The record of the trial does make for interesting reading. Robertson was exonerated.

[2] *The Christadelphian*, 1889, p. 138.

[3] *The Advocate*, 1923 p. 95.

[4] *The Christadelphian*, 1896, p. 476.

[5] *The Boston Globe*, 3 Aug 1896, p. 10.

[6] Engraving from *San Francisco Call*, Saturday, September 24, 1898.

JOB'S QUEST

WRITTEN BY ETHEL ARCHARD

SOONER or later, every Christian comes to Job. It's one of the most unique books of the Bible and one of the most intriguing—an often-perplexing story of how God relates to man. It is one of the most dramatic stories in the Bible, and it's in this dramatic theme that Sis. Ethel Archard (Ottawa Ecclesia, Canada) approaches the narrative. Sis. Ethel advances the idea that "The entire book of Job is written in the form of a drama."

Following the theme of a drama, Sis. Ethel lays it out as a play in three acts and introduces us to the characters, their arguments, and attitudes, concluding with the Divine perspective.

Acknowledging that "The Book of Job is an enigma," Sis. Ethel begins with:

> The meaning of the book of Job is much more complex than it may seem. This inspired literary masterpiece has intrigued Bible students for millennia. It touches on universal themes that were as relevant to the ancients as they are to individual believers today.

We quickly get to the heart of the book:

> What happens to Job becomes the basis for an exploration of God's relationship with His creation. Its truth lies in Job's spiritual transformation.

Along with examining the different roles in the drama, Sis. Ethel introduces us to the chiastic structure helping explain the central message of the book. She writes of Elihu:

> Seen through the lens of the book's chiastic structure, his words bring us closer to right thinking. While still giving a human perspective, Elihu's role is a bridge to the words of Yahweh Himself.

Many of the questions that haunt readers of Job revolve around the role of Satan and God's relationship with him. Sis. Ethel wrestles with several of these questions and helps to put them in a proper perspective for correct understanding.

Job's Quest truly resonated with me when we got to the section entitled "Is God Fair?" To me, this is the cause of much concern and confusion. Sis. Ethel addresses it by writing:

> The debate at the heart of the book revolves around the retributive justice doctrine: God punishes bad people with trouble in this life and rewards good people with health and prosperity. The premise is that God deals with humanity solely on the basis of justice. He has great power, and uses it to reward good people and punish bad people in this life. In other words, God is fair—above all else. You always get what you deserve. The worse the sin, the worse the punishment. By that reasoning, Job must be very sinful to deserve such awful losses and pain!

Sis. Ethel goes beyond the arguments and helps us to connect Job's story to our own personal stories emotionally. As she writes, "Put yourself in Job's shoes because this is a story about real human experience."

I would suggest the same advice. Put yourself in Job's shoes for a while. Spend some time reflecting on the lessons he learned. This book will help you connect to that enigmatic story in a way that might help you more than you imagined. I recommend Job's Quest.

Jeff Gelineau,
(Simi Hills Ecclesia, CA)

Correction: In the September issue (New Market Street Sunday School), we misspelled Bro. Trimal Accra's name. Our apologies.

THE EXCITING WORK IN HAITI

By Steve Johnson

ESMATH Sanival was planning to be a Protestant minister in Haiti. He graduated from a seminary in the Haitian capital city of Port au Prince and began working as an Assistant Pastor. But as he continued his Bible study, he came to the realization that Jesus is not God, the Holy Spirit is not the third person of a trinity, man does not have an immortal soul, and the future true Christian hope is the resurrection from the dead and being part of the Kingdom of God on earth. The only first principle he needed help understanding was the true meaning of the Devil and Satan, and a Christadelphian website helped him understand Bible teaching on this fundamental subject.

Esmath couldn't wait to share his discoveries. People start churches in Haiti simply by finding a space and inviting people in the neighborhood to come. Esmath's meeting began with family members and quickly expanded as they brought friends. One of his appeals was that, unlike other churches in Haiti, Esmath spoke out against tithing, maintaining that the gospel

Bro. Esmath on a Sunday Morning

should be free. He supported himself with a contract job with the UN in Port au Prince. Regular classes were begun using the BASF as a guide and CBMC-supplied French language teaching materials. The meeting began to grow.

In 2009, Bro. Esmath established a small ecclesia under a canopy in a courtyard. About this time, the *Christadelphian Meal-a-Day Fund of the Americas* was established. A friend of one of the Meal-a-Day directors introduced him to Esmath, who, in the aftermath of the 2010 Haiti earthquake, wanted to

Typical scene in Haiti

start a much-needed primary school. Meal-a-Day began funding a school in 2011 and in 2012 moved to a larger rented building that could also serve the growing ecclesia that now, thirteen years later, numbers more than 125 baptized, with many more attending services and studying.

The PEACE Project in Haiti (peaceprojecthaiti.org) was started by a Meal-a-Day director to address and oversee Haiti projects specifically. In addition, a separate preaching organization was formed called "Red Wagon Outreach." The name came from a talk that likened faith to a red Radio Flyer wagon that one needs to get into every day and push forward. Only then can Jesus direct the forward movement by creating obstacles indicating a need for a change in direction.

PEACE Project has been tremendously blessed and is building earthquake-proof and hurricane-hardened steel buildings for the Meal-a-Day funded schools. The ecclesia will utilize these

PEACE Project has been tremendously blessed and is building earthquake proof and hurricane-hardened steel buildings for the Meal-a-Day funded schools.

during non-school hours. The all-purpose building will seat 350 and will be the base for regular Bible conferences. Many members bring interested friends to church services, and so the Truth is introduced to a growing number of people.

COVID-19 has changed the work in Haiti significantly. Two years ago, Bro. Dave Jennings was scheduled to present a day-long Bible seminar at a local, traditional Christian church in Haiti when the pandemic hit. The trip was canceled, and the Christadelphian organizers quickly left the island. Two days later, the Port au Prince airport was closed for months to control the pandemic.

Following on the heels of the pandemic was a growth of instability in Haiti caused by a weak government and the growing control of the country by well-armed gangs. This makes working in Haiti problematic. But what then of Matthew 25: "I lived in Haiti, and you visited me."?

One of the benefits of the pandemic has been the development of the computer program "Zoom." Earlier this year, Red Wagon Outreach tested the idea of bringing outside speakers to Haiti through Zoom by holding a two-session seminar for the leaders of four local churches and the Carrefour Ecclesia.

Bro. Craig Blewett in South Africa gave two classes on "God's Master Plan" to twenty-five people in Haiti. The Q&A was particularly well received. The technology worked flawlessly.

On the basis of this successful test, Bro. Dave Jennings presented to the Haiti church on August 20, 2022. The presentation was extremely well received. Of the one hundred attendees, five people signed up for further

Recent Zoom Conference with Bro. Dave Jennings speaking and Bro. Obed Arris translating

> ## They have a strong need for God and Jesus, with a thirst we rarely see in our prosperous countries.

contact, and plans are being made for more similar Bible conferences at Carrefour churches that have invited us to present "carte blanche" to their congregations. The CBMC supported this preaching effort, and Red Wagon Outreach is hoping that an ongoing relationship will develop. PEACE Project and Meal a Day have developed a great reputation in the community with the three schools supported, an agricultural support program, a vocational school, and medical mission trips to rural areas. It is a "touch and teach" model developed in South Africa. As many as five churches are ready to hold Bible conferences with the understanding that Christadelphians can present whatever content we want to their congregations.

Why are so many people interested in listening to Bible talks all morning in the heat in Haiti? There is usually no electricity in this part of Haiti. Consequently, there are no distractions. The churches have generators so computers and projectors can be run.

Haitians feel the need for God and Jesus in a way we only experience when catastrophes happen in North America. Calamity is a daily experience (or just around the corner) for them. They have a strong need for God and Jesus, with a thirst we rarely see in our prosperous countries. Most of us are getting a taste of the Kingdom now. Haitian brothers and sisters instead struggle daily with survival issues. There is kidnapping for ransom, food and fuel insecurity, health issues and getting any treatment, affordable education for their children (most Haitian schools require tuition), and random gang violence. They truly praise the LORD for His deliverance and sustenance.

Truly the fields in Haiti are white for harvest. You can make a huge difference through your donations. Please visit peaceprojecthaiti.org for how your donation can further enable this good work.

Steve Johnson,
(Bloomington Ecclesia, IL)

Sunday morning in Haiti

Where is Home?

WHERE is home? Is it a physical location? A place where the post office delivers our mail? A place where we keep our clothes, where we return at the end of a workday or a school day? Or is home much more than that?

Jennifer Worth was a midwife who spent her life caring for pregnant women. Delivering their babies was only part of what she did; she also counseled them before and after and helped them along their way through life. She wrote several books chronicling her life and experiences under the title, *Call the Midwife*.[1] Here is how she described a home:

> So where in the end do we belong? In the eyes of another, where we see ourselves reflected, arm in arm with those whose faces echo ours and whose blood we share? Or is it in the heart of the family we create, where we are safest and best known and never lonely?

> Perhaps we belong where love can bloom when we give it room to put down roots and space in which to thrive. Seeds fly in upon the wind and settle where they will. We all belong somewhere. If we are not nurtured where we should be, we must find a choice to make, a place to go, a harbor where the storm is held at bay.

> Sometimes simply belonging to each other is enough. What matters most is not the struggle but where we find our peace.

Home is where we belong and where we feel safe. Not surprisingly, home is where our **real** family is. Robert Frost writes, "Home is the place where, when you have to go there, they have to take you in."[2] And, like Jennifer Worth, he got that right.

But while the ideal of a family starts with common genes, there are times when that commonality is not enough. A person must feel that they belong, and if those with whom they share ancestors treat them like they don't belong, then they may seek a home and a family elsewhere.

"Literature is filled with stories of returning home."

Literature is filled with stories of returning home. Young men leave home and venture out into an unfamiliar world in search of elusive fame, fortune, adventure, and love. Sometimes they succeed, sometimes they fail abysmally, but at the end of their journeys, they always return home, either to the home they left behind or to a better home they have created. They will recognize their real home when they feel safe, at peace, and loved.

The story of the Bible is, among other

things, the story of returning home. Adam and Eve started their lives in a lovely garden where they were protected and cared for and had the best companionship imaginable—the angels of Almighty God. But a serious mistake led to their banishment from the Garden of Eden into a cruel and unforgiving world where life was an unending struggle to protect and feed themselves, and death was a guaranteed end. But at the same time, the LORD God gave them a wonderful hope that one day they might find their way back to the beautiful garden with its tree of life and divine fellowship.

Throughout the Bible, individuals, as well as whole nations, have sought to find their way back home to the presence of God. In the Old Testament, Jews and believers from other nations have found "home," first in the altars and offerings to the LORD individually, later in the Tabernacle in the wilderness, and finally in the great temple at Jerusalem. Others, prophets and wise men, have sought the LORD while in the desert or in the emptiness of mountains, the rest of the world being left behind, and with the voice of God speaking directly to them. Finally, in later days, others have found their true home under the sheltering arms of a Messiah, a Savior, Jesus Christ, the Son of God.

While traveling through the land of Canaan, Jacob had a vision one night of angels ascending to and from heaven. At the same time, he received a revelation from God, reaffirming to him the promises of eternal blessings and inheritance in the Land of

Promise God had made to Abraham. This led Jacob to name the place "*Bethel*," that is, the House of God (Gen 35:14, 15). In his wanderings, Jacob had found his special home in the promises of God.

Moses was a man of God, a leader of his people, and a prophet. In Psalm 90 (often attributed to Moses), he prays:

> LORD *you have been our dwelling place throughout all generations… Satisfy us in the morning with your unfailing love, that we may sing for joy and be glad all our days* (v. 1, 14).[3]

All his life, Moses had lived in alien places like Egypt, or temporary stopovers in a vast wilderness, on a journey that never seemed to end. At the age of 120, he finally died after he glimpsed in the distance the long-sought Promised Land. But that brief look was enough; Moses had dwelt with God throughout his life and finally had seen God's special Land, which would be his eternal dwelling place.

Ruth, a young widow with no children, left Moab, the land of her birth, but found a new home with her mother-in-law Naomi in Bethlehem. Ruth told her:

> *Don't urge me to leave you or to turn back from you. Where you go I will go, and where you stay I will stay. Your people will be my people and your God my God.*" (Ruth 1:16).

With her new home, she found her share through the promises of her new god, the God of Israel. She also found a redeemer husband, Boaz, with whom she had a child who would become an ancestor of the Lord Jesus Christ (Matt 1:5, 16). Her new family gave her all she could ever have imagined in this life and every hope of a more glorious life yet to come in the Kingdom of God.

Our ecclesia should be our home, our family, and our refuge. It should not be a place of judgment, argument, or gossip, but sometimes it is. In a world filled with pain, suffering, and loss, the ecclesia should be a place of comfort and peace—and a place of belonging, of feeling safe, and of enveloping love.

Sometimes, however, the ecclesia may fail us. Sometimes, sadly, we may fail the ecclesia. But we can all try again, over and over, to love one another, just as our Savior has loved us:

> *Dear friends, since God so loved us, we also ought to love one another.* (1 John 4:11).

George Booker,
(Austin Leander Ecclesia, TX)

---

[1] Worth, Jennifer, *Call the Midwife*, Penguin Books, 375 Hudson Street, New York City, NY, 2002.

[2] Frost, Robert, *The Death of the Hired Man*.

[3] All Scriptural citations are taken from the *New International Version*.

THE CHRISTADELPHIAN
TIDINGS
OF THE KINGDOM OF GOD

is published monthly, except bimonthly in July-August, by The **Christadelphian Tidings**, 567 Astorian Drive, Simi Valley, CA 93065-5941. **FIRST CLASS POSTAGE PAID** at Simi Valley, CA and at additional mailing offices. POSTMASTER: Send address changes to The Christadelphian Tidings, 567 Astorian Dr., Simi Valley, CA 93065.

Christadelphian Tidings Publishing Committee: Alan Markwith (Chairman), Joe Hill, John Bilello, Peter Bilello, Linda Beckerson, Nancy Brinkerhoff, Shawn Moynihan, Kevin Flatley, Jeff Gelineau, William Link, and Ken Sommerville.

Christadelphian Tidings Editorial Committee: Dave Jennings (Editor), Section Editors: Nathan Badger (Life Application), TBA (Exhortation and Consolation), Jessica Gelineau (Music and Praise), Steve Cheetham (Exposition), Richard Morgan (First Principles), Dave Jennings (Teaching and Preaching), Jan Berneau (CBMA/C), George Booker, (Thoughts on the Way, Q&A), John Bilello (Letters to the Editor), Jeff Gelineau (News and Notices, Subscriptions), Melinda Flatley (Writer Recruitment and Final Copy), and Shawn Moynihan (Books).

Subscriptions: The Tidings Magazine is provided **FREE** for any who would like to read it. The Magazine is available in PDF Format online at **tidings.org**. If you would like to order a printed subscription to **The Tidings** you may do so simply by making a donation to cover the printing costs. The Suggested Donation for printing and shipping is **USD $50.00;** (we ask for a Minimum Donation of USD $25.00 for a printed subscription.)

All subscription information is available online at **www.tidings.org**. You may subscribe online and make donations online or by mail to the above address. Information on how to subscribe in other countires is also available online at **www.tidings.org/subscribe**.

The Christadelphian Tidings is published on the 15th of the month for the month following. Items for publication must be received by the 1st of the month. Correspondence to the editor, Dave Jennings at **editor@tidings.org**. Publication of articles does not presume editorial endorsement except on matters of fundamental doctrine as set forth in the BASF. Letters should be sent via e-mail to **letters@tidings.org**. Please include your name, address and phone number. The magazine reserves the right to edit all submissions for length and clarity.

Made in the USA
Columbia, SC
24 September 2022

67501175R00033